1956	Elvis releases "Heartbreak Hotel"
1964	The Beatles conquer America
1969	Woodstock Festival
1975	Queen release "Bohemian Rhapsody"
1977	Sex Pistols banned from BBC
1981	Bucks Fizz win Eurovision Song Contest
1989	Jive Bunny ruins 12 songs on one record
1993	Mr. Blobby goes in at No. 1
2001	Hear'Say manufactured
2002	Hear'Say disintegrate
2007	First digitally created cyber-star tops chart
2009	Ugly people banned from chart
2021	Kids require a licence to own an electric guitar
2030	Radio 1 plays last non-computer-created tune
2046	ALL MUSICAL INSTRUMENTS BANNED

WE WILL ROCK YOU

The MUSICAL by QUEEN and Ben Elton

THE OFFICIAL BOOK including **SCRIPT** and **FULL LYRICS** to all songs

Original London Production

Foreword by **Brian May** and **Roger Taylor**

CARLTON
BOOKS

Phil McIntyre, Queen Theatrical Productions and Tribeca Theatrical Productions

in association with

EMI, Paul Roberts, Michael Watt, Michael Coppel

present

Music and Lyrics

Queen

Story and Script and Directed by

Ben Elton

This is a Carlton book

First published in Great Britain in 2004
by Carlton Books Limited
20 Mortimer Street
London W1T 3JW

Script, photography and logo © Queen Productions Limited
Design and introductory text © Carlton Books Limited 2004

This version edited by Brian May, authorised by Ben Elton.
Acknowledgements to Liz Akers and Peter Gibbon-Hansen for
help in compiling, and Jennifer Tunney for proof reading.

Lyrics reproduced by kind permission.

ISBN 1 84442 825 7

Design consultant: Richard Gray
Introduction by Ian Gittins

Project Editor: Lorna Russell

Art Director: Jeremy Southgate

Cover design: Karin Fremer

Front cover photograph: George Bodnor/Dewynters
Production: Lisa Moore

The publishers would like to thank the following sources for
their kind permission to reproduce the pictures in this book:
Catherine Ashmore/p16t, 20, 21, 22, 23, 32, 33, 43,86, 94/95, 97,
114/115; Dave Benett/p13t, 16b, 24, 28, 29, 35, 36, 160b;
Tim Goodchild/p14, 15; Richard Gray/p11, 13b, 18, 19, 38,
40, 42,44, 46, 47, 49, 50, 51, 52,53, 54, 55, 57, 58, 59, 61, 62,
65 67, m68, 69, 70/71, 72/73, 74, 76, 77, 79, 80/81, 83, 84, 85,
87, 88, 90, 91, 92, 93, 98, 100, 103,105, 106, 107,109, 110,
112,113, 116, 117, 118, 119, 120, 121, 123, 124, 126, 128, 130,
132, 133, 136, 137, 139, 141, 142, 143, 145, 146/147, 148,149,
152, 153, 154, 155, 156, 157, 158/159. Curtain photo throughout.
Stage designs: Mark Fisher
We Will Rock You logo designed by Dwynters, London
Every effort has been made to acknowledge correctly and contact
the source and/or copyright holder of each picture, and Carlton
Books Limited apologises for any unintentional errors or omissions
which will be corrected in future editions of this book.

The Official International Queen Fan Club, 16a Barnes High Street,
London SW13 9LW
www.queenworld.com

Contents

ORIGINAL LONDON CAST
(in order of appearance)

Pop	Nigel Planer
Khashoggi	Alexander Hanson/Clive Carter
Galileo	Tony Vincent
Scaramouche	Hannah Jane Fox
Killer Queen	Sharon D Clarke
Britney	Nigel Clauzel
Meat	Kerry Ellis

BAND

Music Director & Piano Mike Dixon

Associate Music Director/Keyboard Andy Smith

Keyboard Spike Edney

Keyboard/Synthesiser Programming Jeff Leach

Guitar Laurie Wisefield

Guitar Alan Darby

Bass Guitar Neil Murray

Drums Tony Bourke

Percussion Julian Poole

THE ENSEMBLE
(in alphabetical order)

Sam Archer

Giorgia Barberi

Luke Baxter

Lucy Williamson/
Mazz Murray   (Teacher)

Nick Crossley

Alistair David

Andrew Derbyshire

Lucie Fentum

Amy Field

Taira Foo

Amanda Harrison

Dalh Haynes

Cameron Jack

Jenna Lee-James

Chris Lennon

Giles New (Big Macca)

Zak Nermorin

Laetitia Ray

Richard Roe

Golda Rosheuvel

Nicola Stuart

Leon Webster

UNDERSTUDIES

Pop	Giles New
	Luke Baxter
Khashoggi	Luke Baxter
	Cameron Jack
Galileo	Andrew Derbyshire
	Chris Lennon
Scaramouche	Jenna Lee-James
	Amanda Harrison
Killer Queen	Mazz Murray
	Golda Rosheuvel
	Lucy Williamson
Britney	Cameron Jack
	Chris Lennon
Meat	Amanda Harrison
	Lucie Fentum
Teacher	Golda Rosheuvel
	Lucie Fentum
Big Macca	Chris Lennon
	Richard Roe
	Andrew Derbyshire

SWINGS (in alphabetical order)

Bekki Chana

Mark Marson

Robert Ricks

Tania Robb

Phong Truong

Anna Woodside

PRODUCTION TEAM

Director	Ben Elton
Production Designer	Mark Fisher
Lighting Designer	Willie Williams
Video Directors	Mark Fisher & Willie Williams
Sound Designer	Bobby Aitken
Costume Designer	Tim Goodchild
Casting Director	Pippa Ailion
US Casting	Bernard Tesley Casting
Resident Director	Tony Edge
Assistant Choreographer	Lucie Pankhurst
Resident Choreographer	John Clarke
Vocal Harmony Arrangements	Brian May & Mike Dixon
Orchestrator	Steve Sidwell
Music Supervisors	Mike Dixon, Brian May & Roger Taylor
Musical Staging & Choreography	Arelene Phillips
Director of Original London Production	Christopher Renshaw
Company Manager	Peter Gibbon/Hansen
Stage Manager	David Curl
Deputy Stage Manager	Tracy-Ann Ransom
Assistant Stage Manager	Jessica Ashmore-Short
Assistant Stage Manager	Abbie Gingell
Assistant Stage Manager	Ian Shillito
Assistant Stage Manager	Dave West
Sound No 1	Simon Sayer
Sound No 2	Emma Sainsbury
Sound No 3	Ben Milton
Sound No 4	Richard Stott
Wardrobe Master	Duncan Newman
Deputy Wardrobe Mistress	Sarah Sharp
Wardrobe Assistant	Wendy Phillips
Wig Mistress	Sue Strother
Wig Deputy	Helen Bowner
Wig Assistant	Fadil Abdelhadi/ Katie Marson
Crew Chief	Kieran McGivern
Deputy Crew Chief	Luke Fraser
Head Flyman	Edward Forbes
Chief Electrician	Matt Barker
Deputy Electrician/ Board Operator	Rik Cochrane
Video HoD	Gary Rhodes
Video Chief No 1	Bob Kronman
Video No 2	Dominic Clements

for WE WILL ROCK YOU (LONDON)

Manager	Ted Irwin
Co-ordinator	Liz Akers
Accounts	John McIntyre
Costume Supervisor	Joy Bondini
Hair, Wig & Make-up Supervision	Campbell Young
Technical Design Assistant	Piers Shepperd
Associate Lighting Designer	Bruce Ramus
Theatre Lighting Associate	Michael Odam
Theatre Lighting Assistant	Pete Lambert
Assistant Sound Designer	Richard Sharratt
Assistant Costume Designer	Samantha Crockett
Assistant Costume, Hair, Wig and Make-up	Chris Redman
Production Costume Assistant	Jo Worsley
Additional Audio Pre-production	Joshua J Macrae
Additional Audio Pre-production	Justin Shirley-Smith
Additional Audio Pre-production	Kris Fredriksson
Computer Animation	Adrian Mudd at the Mark Fisher Studio
Video Production Facility	Mark Logue & Marina Fiorato at Punk Films
Control Engineer	Peter Didier
Chief Production Electrician	Gerry Amies
Production Electrician	Martin Chisnell
Production Electrician	Ian Moulds
Production Electrician	Ron Beattie
Production Electrician	Greg Hamlin
Moving Light Programmer	Patrick Murray
Chief Production Sound Engineer	Ali Viles
Production Sound Engineer	Martin Dinely
Production Sound Engineer	Simon Hodge
Production Sound Engineer	Stewart Chaney
Head Production Carpenter	Andy Chelton
Production Carpenter	Bob Fitsimmons
Production Carpenter	Martin Gelder
Production Carpenter	Alex Rich
Video Programmer	Richard Turner
Assistant to Brian May	Sara Bricusse/Sally Frost
Assistant to Roger Taylor	Justine Ellis-Morris
Assistant to Jim Beach	Anne Meyer
Assistant to Jane Rosenthal	Meghan Lyvers
Assistant to Mark Fisher	Gillian Ward
Assistant to Christopher Renshaw	Christian Durham
Assistant to Arlene Phillips	Rebecca Bennett
Assistant to Ted Irwin	Zoe Gauld
Assistant Casting Director	Louise Townshend
US Casting Associate	Craig Burns
Musicians Contractor	Sylvia Addison at Music Solutions
Music Preparations	Richard Sidwell
Musician Auditions Co-ordinator	Martin Groves
Road Crew & Gear Co-ordinator	Pete Malandrone
Rehearsal Pianist	Dave Adams
Audition Stage Manager	John Taylor
Audition Stage Manager	Monique Seif
Legal Services to the Producers	Neil Adelman at Harbottle and Lewis
Legal Services to Queen	Robert Lee at Lee and Thompson

for WE WILL ROCK YOU (LONDON)

Legal Services to Phil McIntyre	*Andrew Ferguson at Napthen Houghton Craven*
Legal Services for Tribeca	*Gil A. Karson & Larry Shire at Grubman Indursky & Schindler*
Accountants	*Michael Collins & Lois Hargreaves for Collins & Company*
Insurance	*Richard Walton at Walton & Parkinson*
Production Photographer	*Catherine Ashmore*
Souvenir Brochure Design	*Richard Gray*
Online Marketing and Production	*Ant Cauchi, Nick Weymouth, Greg Findon, Ben Morris & Greg Viercan for Outside Line*
Advertising and Marketing	*Dewynters, London*
Press Representative	*Phil Symes at The PR Contact*
Queen Management	*Jim Beach*

PRODUCTION CREDITS

Scenery	*Brilliant Stages, Clearwater Scenery, Promptside, Kimpton Walker, Cardiff Theatrical Services, Souvenir, Bowerwood Presentations, Systems Control, Delstar Engineering Ltd, Gerriets GB, Steel Monkey Engineering*
Forestage Engineering Design	*Mike Barnett*
Rigging	*Vertigo Rigging*
Scenery Painting	*Frances Waddington and Friends & Chris Clark*
Props	*Souvenir*
Lighting Equipment	*Stage Electrics*
Additional Electrical Installation	*RWS*
Sound Equipment	*Autograph Sound Recording Ltd*
Video Screens	*Lighthouse Technologies Europe*
Additional Video Equipment	*Blitz Vision*
Laser Effects	*Definitive Special Projects Ltd*
Costume	*Susan Adams, Fran Alderson, Amanda Barrow, Carol Coates, Classic Cuts, Paddie Dickie, Jane Grimshaw, Lil Harrison, Frances Hill, Deborah Marchant, Corinne Noble, Kit Reading, Phil Reynolds, John Sheward*
Wigs	*Campbell Young & Associates, Robert Allsop & Associates, Bodyline*
Printing	*Jamison Print Ltd, Penny Hadrill*
Dyeing	*Nicola Killeen*
Shoes	*Gamba, K&D Shoes*
Assistant Costume Supervisor	*Samantha Crockett*
Dry Cleaning	*Upstage Theatrical Dry Cleaning*
Physiotheraphy	*Sports and Spinal Clinics Fulham, Fabi Waisbord D.O.*
Make-up	*Shu Uemura*
Musical Instruments	*Arbiter UK, John Henry's, Korg Line 6, Rockyroad, Roland UK, Vox Amplifiers*
Drumkit	*Premier Company*
Cymbals	*Zildjian*
Guitars	*B.M. Burns of London, Fryers guitars, Bass Acoustic Centre*

Forewords

We Will Rock You – the Rock Theatrical, as I like to call it – is a dream come
true. We, Queen, searched long and hard for a way to move our music into
the theatre. Sure, Queen played theatres, but the world of musicals
was something almost diametrically opposite to what we were aiming for.
Could we make a musical which really rocked?!
At the point where we had tried the biographical approach, and not found anything we
considered workable, or bearable, just when we were on the verge
of throwing in the towel, Ben Elton provided the key.
He came up with a scenario set in the future which rang so true to our ears, and
so neatly captured the spirit of much of our music, that we instantly agreed to
go for it. Ben spun the magical tale which appears on these pages, which was
to throw us into a journey unlike any before.

Two tumultuous years after we first opened our doors, the show has
become something so close to our hearts, so lovingly nurtured and fiercely guarded by
us, that I cannot imagine life with out it now. *We Will Rock You*,
now flourishing in London, Australia, and Madrid, and soon to blossom in many other
distant climes, has benefited from the talents and ceaseless hard
work of an army of some of the most brilliant young actors, musicians, production
staff and technicians in the world today. Our dream has become
theirs too, and to them, our wonderful team, this book of words is dedicated.

Rock On!!!

With Love,
Brian

I've never liked musicals!
It always seemed daft when the dialogue stopped and
people burst into song for seemingly no reason at all.
I love this one; because it makes people laugh and,
above all, it rocks.

Roger Taylor

"IT'S A KIND OF MAGIC..."

Interviewed in this account by Ian Gittins, Ben Elton, the author of the spectacular show, explains how he came to create the play that is likely to become the most successful rock musical in history – and looks set to run and run.

Ever since it opened its doors at London's Dominion Theatre in May 2002, the magnificent *We Will Rock You* has played to packed evening and matinée houses at the 2,200-seater West End venue. As thousands of fans continue to flock through the doors, the show is well on its way to becoming the most successful musical in history – a truly staggering achievement.

The show's success, moreover, isn't limited to the UK. *We Will Rock You* also opened to rave reviews in Melbourne, Australia, where it has similarly proven a huge success. Further productions in Spain and the US are also underway, and they certainly won't be the last. The magic of Queen, after all, is universal – and global.

So how did *We Will Rock You* come about? The story, as would maybe be expected, is a long and complex one, but with a decidedly happy ending.

Based on the music of the legendary rock titans Queen, the show's script was penned by Ben Elton, the London-based author and comic writer whose career achievements include eight best-selling novels as well as many iconic, British TV series including *The Young Ones* and *Blackadder*. Ben's previous theatre projects have included three West End hits plus his collaboration with Andrew Lloyd Webber, *The Beautiful Game*, which won the London Critics' Circle Award for Best New Musical in 2000.

A Queen fan since he was a boy, Ben freely admits that it was not his idea to turn the band's extraordinary back catalogue into a dramatic stage musical. Rather, the original credit lies with Jim Beach, Queen's long-standing but forward-thinking manager. Jim and Queen had been

toying with the idea of adapting Queen's exhaustive collection for a theatrical format since the mid-nineties. Originally, they had considered using the songs to tell the life story of the band's flamboyant singer, Freddie Mercury, who died tragically young in 1991.

"I got a call some time during 2000 from Paul Roberts, from the production company Phil McIntyre Productions," Ben explains. "He said to me, 'Queen would like to meet you, because they want to do a stage musical and would like you to write the story and the script.' Naturally, I was very flattered and enthusiastic by this information. Who wouldn't be?

"I've wondered a few times since whether Paul wasn't pulling a little producer's trick, and telling Queen at the same time, 'Would you like to meet Ben Elton, because he'd like to write a musical based on your songs?' Well, if he was pulling a fast one, it certainly worked, because I met up with Jim Beach, and then with Queen themselves."

Queen's manager explained to Ben that Robert De Niro's New York production company Tribeca had started work on a possible Queen musical, but had decided that the script they were working with was unsatisfactory. He asked Ben whether he would like to attempt to develop this original script or else write a completely fresh treatment based on a biography of Freddie. Ben Elton wasn't keen on either idea.

"I didn't think it was the right idea to base a Queen musical on Freddie's life," he says. "Freddie was a great, great artist before his tragically early death, but Queen are more than just Freddie. Their music doesn't chronicle his life and they don't pretend that it does. A Queen musical needs to reflect the entire band.

"Queen are uniquely theatrical and their music is operatic, choral and full of wit. The lyrics are huge and portentous, and the band has a truly legendary quality. So I told Jim Beach that I didn't think their music suited a naturalistic biography such as the story of Freddie, and he said, 'Fair enough – but let us know if you have any other ideas for it.'"

The manager and the writer went separate ways and would have no further contact for a full year. During this time, Ben Elton continued to

OPPOSITE TOP: Scaramouche (Hannah Jane Fox) and Galileo (Tony Vincent) performing at the premiere
OPPOSITE BOTTOM: Killer Queen (Sharon D Clarke) and Khashoggi (Clive Carter)

ponder possible plot lines for the production. He knew intuitively that, to match the unique grandeur of Queen's music, the story would need to be implausible, larger than life, magnificent and somehow . . . heroic.

"I saw *The Matrix*, and the idea of a world where a computer runs everything and the people are just cogs in the wheel was on my mind," he recalls. "I wanted something legendary, and even toyed with the notion of setting the King Arthur legend to Queen songs. I was idly playing with those ideas one day as I was pushing my kids in their pram through Regents Park, and the whole storyline of *We Will Rock You* just came to me from nowhere.

"I suddenly imagined this world where rock music is banned and the kids are oppressed by computerized pop, and there is this ridiculous, overblown legend of guitars being secretly buried in a secret location. Don't ask me how, but I went out that afternoon with an empty mind and came back with the entire plot of *We Will Rock You*. I ran home, wrote it down immediately, and sent it to Queen."

It was clearly a remarkable epiphany, since the plot has remained relatively unaltered since that fateful walk in the park.

The story of *We Will Rock You*, at heart, is a simple one. Deep into the twenty-first century, the Earth – now renamed Planet Mall – is

Original drawings showing costume designs for the Bohemians and the Ga Ga girls

homogenized beyond belief. Globalisation has taken its toll. In particular, a vast corporation named Globalsoft monopolises popular culture. Citizens are forced to download its anodyne tunes, composed by computer, from the internet. Musical instruments are banned.

Resistance, it seems, is futile until the emergence of Galileo and Scaramouche, two unhappy but idealistic teenagers. The shy Galileo, shunned by his peers, 'hears' lines and words from classic rock tunes in his head, and suspects that a great destiny awaits him. The initially sullen and suspicious Scaramouche becomes his girlfriend, and the star-crossed lovers tackle the tyranny of Globalsoft head-on.

"All musicals, and all good stories, are essentially love stories," develops Ben. "With *We Will Rock You*, I was intrigued by the idea of two punk rebels against the world. Galileo and Scaramouche are archetypal teenagers, real James Dean, rebel-without-a-cause types, two loners and outsiders who get bullied at school. They dress in black and they hate fashion yet, at heart, they're very attractive characters."

Given the conceptual green light from Queen, via Jim Beach, Ben retired to his study and set about the mammoth task of fleshing out his initial plot premise into a fully detailed script and weaving hits

We Will Rock You It's A Kind of Magic

from Queen's extensive repertoire into the futuristic storyline.

"It was unlike any other writing job I'd ever taken on, because it involved working very closely with a hugely successful, monumental body of work in Queen's songs," he says. "Obviously I was aware how much they mean to a lot of people, and that was an intimidating prospect in itself. I mean, I was nine when 'Bohemian Rhapsody' went to Number One. I've always loved Queen.

"The unique thing about the group, to me, is how universally liked they are. They've never been painfully unhip. Initially, they had a foot in the glam thing, like David Bowie, but even when punk rock came along and a lot of long-standing bands got slaughtered, Queen were OK because they were up for a laugh. They had a big sense of humour and they took the piss out of themselves and never took themselves too seriously. For my part, I just thought, 'Great! What an unbelievable opportunity to work with these songs that mean a lot to me anyway.'

"At my first meeting with Queen, Brian May said to me, 'You've got to become a member of Queen. That means we can give you compliments, like, "We love your synopsis." But we can also tell you if we have problems with your script.' I was fine with that kind of honesty, and that's how we approached the project. Luckily, I have a fair degree of confidence when I write."

Ben's writing flowed easily during the early stages, but he was forced to rethink some of his ideas when the band decided he had taken too many creative liberties with their songs.

"A lot of the ideas and the song placements that occurred to me that day in the park have stayed the same, and were very simple to write down," he says. "However, I did find myself tampering with the lyrics quite a lot to help the songs to fit into the story more easily. I thought I'd use a bit of poetic licence.

"Then I took my first draft of the script to Brian and Roger [Taylor], and they told me – quite correctly, I think now – 'This is madness. We want a

OPPOSITE TOP: Ben Elton, Brian May and Roger Taylor deep in discussion in the early stages of the show's development ...
OPPOSITE BOTTOM: ... and appearing on stage to rapturous applause at the end of Premiere

musical of our songs, not a total rewrite of them.' At which point I realised, it doesn't matter if not every single line of every song fits the plot. It's the vibe of the song that counts in the end." Hands-on and involved throughout the whole project, Brian May and Roger Taylor were vocal in their thoughts on Ben's first draft script. The Queen duo examined the list of songs he intended to include and suggested additions and revisions. With their intimate knowledge of the songs they had created and then performed for decades, Brian and Roger helped to schedule the songs to facilitate the story's emotional musical journey.

"Brian and Roger worked really hard with me on the placement of the songs," explains Ben. "A lot got moved around as the dramatic contribution of the music to the plot became more central. Plus, of course, they handled all of the orchestrations, harmonies and choruses, and ensured the music really captured all of the energised passion we were trying to convey."

Brian and Roger also helped Ben develop certain passages of the script that he had initially found somewhat thorny. Originally, Ben had envisaged that the buried guitar, pursued like a Holy Grail by Galileo and Scaramouche, should be found at Stonehenge, until the Queen members gently suggested that this particular location was possibly "a little bit too *Spinal Tap.*"

"Brian very cleverly pointed out that there is a real-life statue of Freddie Mercury by Lake Geneva, in Switzerland," explains Ben. "He suggested we could locate the Place of the Living Rock there, and even have the Seven Seas of Rhye flowing into the lake! It was a brilliant idea, but I didn't think Switzerland was quite rock'n'roll enough for the play's dénouement.

"However, Brian's brainwave did give me the idea of Galileo and Scaramouche finding the statue of Freddie which could be pointing towards the true Place of the Living Rock – Wembley, where Freddie and Queen played so many times. We invented the Legend of the Bright Star, and after that, the rest of the plot just fell neatly into place."

Only a few of Ben Elton's original lyrical re-writes survived the scrutiny of Brian and Roger, but the ones that did are notable. "Killer Queen", sung in *We Will Rock You* by the

Globalsoft matriarch of the same name, references email and the internet – home technology that was unimaginable when Freddie Mercury wrote the song back in 1974. Largely, though, Brian and Roger had made Ben realise that he had to tailor his outrageous storyline to the songs, rather than vice versa.

"I found the writing a joy, really" he reflects. "There were so many natural synergies. In one scene when Scaramouche is distraught, oppressed and suppressed and looking for a way out, it was obvious that she should sing 'Somebody To Love'. Galileo singing 'I Want To Break Free' also made total sense. They are the two leads, and I think they're the best characters and the ones I most enjoyed writing.

"If I had to choose one character I'm fondest of, it would be Scaramouche. Basically, I'm a relatively benign, middle-aged man nowadays, so it was obviously a large leap of imagination for me to sit down and attempt to write the part of a grumpy, alienated, teenage girl. That kind of comedy of attitude is very difficult to conceive, but very rewarding when you manage to pull it off."

Ben also perceives interesting parallels between the male lead, Galileo, and Queen's own, original alpha male, Freddie Mercury. "In *We Will Rock You*, when Galileo is at the Virtual High School, he senses that he is different from everyone else but doesn't know why, so he is resentful and cynical," he explains. "I understand that Freddie was also very shy, and always hid it from people by putting on this great show all the time. Only his best friends knew that he was very sensitive and complex beneath it all."

As the writing process drew to a close in mid-2001, Ben felt warily confident that he had succeeded in transferring Queen's opulent, lavish and famously grandiose music into a storyline of fitting splendour and enjoyable absurdity.

"It's ridiculously overblown," he freely confesses, "but hopefully it works." However, audiences can't help but discern a topical undercurrent to the show – a righteous disdain for the current trend of pre-packaged, manufactured, popular culture that is epitomised by TV talent shows such as *Pop Idol*.

FROM LEFT: Meat (Kerry Ellis) and Britney (Nigel Clauzel), Scaramouche (Hannah Jane Fox), Galileo (Tony Vincent) and Pop (Nigel Planer)

Top Left: Nigel Clauzel (Meat), Kerry Ellis (Meat) and Tony Vincent (Galileo)
Top Centre: Rehearsals took place in a disused school in South London
Top Right: Producer Paul Roberts with Roger Taylor

"Obviously, there is a degree of satire in the show," Ben confirms. "There is a serious spine to *We Will Rock You*, and it's that popular entertainment is way too pre-planned nowadays, and global corporations are far too involved in what's in the pop charts and what movies are getting to be made.

"The money involved in marketing is so important that if a record or a film isn't an immediate hit, it's automatically pronounced a flop. In the old days, you'd always know at the end of the summer what that year's blockbuster film had been, because it was the one the public had chosen to go and see. Now we're told in advance what the big hit will be, and it has to do well so that all the merchandising and marketing spin-offs can also succeed and McDonald's can sell loads of little plastic toys.

"It's the same with music. In my day, records used to climb the singles chart slowly to Number One, and it was exciting – 'Will this week's Number One be Bowie, or Slade, or Mud?' Now, if Posh Spice doesn't go straight in at Number One the week her record comes out, she is

deemed a failure and loses her record contract. Once, the only people who debuted at Number One were The Beatles.

"It's silly to say that I hate *Pop Idol* – I don't. I can watch an episode and get caught up in it like anyone else, and I have no problem at all with Will Young or Gareth Gates. Let's face it; there will always be a place in this world for attractive people singing nice ballads. But there is no doubt that *Pop Idol* was part of the fuel that helped me to imagine Ga Ga School and Planet Mall. George Orwell's *1984* was actually about 1948, a satire on his day, and I guess in that respect – although I'd never dare to compare myself with George Orwell – *We Will Rock You* is a satire on today."

Once Ben and Queen had agreed upon the final script, they turned their minds to casting. Brian May and Roger Taylor were once again heavily involved in this aspect of the production, sitting through countless, lengthy audition sessions along with Ben. Naturally, most of the attention was initially focused on the drama's two leading characters: Galileo and Scaramouche.

"Casting is a very complicated job, and it went on forever," says Ben. "Hannah Jane Fox was in the frame for Scaramouche quite early on. It took a lot longer to cast Galileo, but in the end we found him in America,

*Brian, Ben and Roger
worked together closely
on the script*

*The show's Music
Supervisor Mike Dixon
and Brian on keyboards*

in Tony Vincent. There is no question, though, that we found the right people. The lead actors have helped me to create the roles as well as develop them. They've done great work."

It would have been impossible to find a more appropriate Galileo than Tony Vincent, a singer-songwriter who has released three albums for Epic Records US and has appeared in both *Rent* and *Jesus Christ Superstar* in New York. Hannah Jane Fox also relishes the part of the sparky Scaramouche, having previously starred in *Rent*, *Hot Stuff* and *Rocky Horror Show*. At *We Will Rock You*'s rehearsals, she was honoured when Brian May took time out to give her a few air guitar lessons, to ensure that her approximations of Queen's legendary riffs looked stylish and correct!

One major character, however, was exempt from the laborious casting procedure. Pop, the fusty, old librarian and ex-hippie who opens *We Will Rock You* resisting Globalsoft and who is a major fulcrum in the plot, was earmarked for only one actor, from the first stroke of Ben Elton's pen.

"I wanted Nigel Planer, my old mate from *The Young Ones*, to play Pop from the very start," admits Ben. "In fact, I actually wrote the part of Pop with him in mind. He was the only character who was cast before he was even written. Nigel also took part in the very early workshops as I developed the script, and he unsurprisingly turned out to be a superb Pop."

Another casting of note was the redoubtable Sharon D Clarke as the vivacious, compellingly Thatcherite Killer Queen, the head of Globalsoft, who dedicates herself to crushing rebels and deviants beneath her stilettos like so many insects.

"Killer Queen is pretty two-dimensional as characters go," notes Ben. "But I do think that, out of everybody, she's a lot of fun to watch."

When *We Will Rock You* swung into rehearsals at the beginning of 2002, Ben was initially absent due to other work commitments. Instead, Brian May and Roger Taylor attended the majority of rehearsals, suggesting

OPPOSITE TOP: *Galileo (Tony Vincent) and company rock the house at the premiere*
OPPOSITE BOTTOM: *Killer Queen (Sharon D Clarke) and Khashoggi (Clive Carter) take a bow*

changes and overseeing musical amendments until Ben returned to take up the directorial reins. Like all work-in-progress dramas, the script was constantly changing shape.

"At one stage, I introduced a sub-plot, which stayed in the production until just before the play opened," says Ben. "It was written around Galileo and Scaramouche, and the idea was that they would have this split, a setback in the journey that would lead to them falling out before they ended up back together again.

"So I wrote this storyline that involved Scaramouche being captured by Khashoggi, the Globalsoft head of security, and Galileo trying to save her. During his quest, he met up with Meat Loaf – who is not only a woman but also a rock chick in this play! – and he ended up sleeping with her. It was a complicated sub-plot but eventually I realised it didn't work, it was rubbish, and so I dropped it.

"At that point, we went back to the story we'd started with in our workshop, months earlier, and which we should probably have stayed with all along. In any drama, though, these experiments are worth doing. It gave me a few new jokes, and we kept the idea of Galileo and Scaramouche having a big fall-out during the second act, as well as adding the 'Hammer To Fall' sequence. The process of development was entirely organic."

The rehearsals also saw the development of the characters of the Bohemians, the plucky (if confused) band of ageing rockers and punks who live underground while devoting their lives to the overthrow of Globalsoft and the rediscovery of real music and creativity in a future, golden age they call The Rhapsody. Patiently, they await the coming of their Messiah, the visionary figure who will fulfil their dream.

"They realize Galileo is the one they've been waiting for before he even knows that himself," says Ben. "But because they only know real music second-hand, from historical accounts, they get it all wrong: you get these bikers and rockers calling themselves Britney Spears and Cliff Richard, or Bob The Builder, and rock chicks called Meat Loaf . . . "

Through the painful but productive rehearsal process, Ben, Brian and Roger slowly began to realize that they had something very special on their hands. Although a few of the more ambitious staging directions had to be abandoned ("We had to accept that we were in a theatre, not a stadium," admits Ben), *We Will Rock You* was still clearly a vast and spectacular production. Nevertheless, there was more to it than this. The script, to everyone's delight, turned out to be sharp, witty and very funny.

"I was amazed that even at the first preview show, everything went really well," says Ben. "The joy was that the comedy 'landed', as we say in the theatre, which basically means that the jokes got laughs immediately. When you are rehearsing any show, there's always an awful point a few weeks in when you start to wonder, 'Is any of this funny? Does it make sense at all?' Within two or three days of the preview shows, we started getting standing ovations. Everything was looking fantastic.

"That doesn't mean we weren't still changing things. We altered the production quite radically in various ways during the preview shows, although the audiences seemed to love it all the same. There were some problems to do with getting actors on and off stage at the right time, and the only way to tackle it was to see what worked and what didn't. But we put everything right.

"We also introduced an element that may have looked a bit corny, a bit panto, but which really works. The play originally ended with 'We Are The Champions' outside Wembley, and then after the applause died down, we were playing 'Bohemian Rhapsody', which is still Queen's greatest song, as a bonus, almost like an encore at a rock show. One night during a preview, I said, 'Why not bring "Bo Rap" in by asking the crowd, "Do you want to hear 'Bohemian Rhapsody'?"' We thought it might be a bit naff, but we tried it – and the audience roars took the roof off the theatre. They still do, every single night."

We Will Rock You finally launched at the London Dominion on Tuesday, May 14, 2002 in front of a stellar audience. Sir Richard Branson, Chris Tarrant, Sir Tim Rice, Jamie Oliver, Stephen Berkoff, Ulrika Jonsson and even Donny Osmond, were among the host of showbiz names who gathered for the première, although the world's media were most excited by the presence of Robert De Niro, who had remained a major backer of the show.

One earnest journalist asked De Niro the difference between *We Will Rock You* and any other production he'd been involved in. "This one's got songs in it," deadpanned the laconic Hollywood icon, to appreciative chuckles.

Top Left: Ben Elton, Robert De Niro, Brian May and Roger Taylor at the We Will Rock You press conference
Top Centre: Tony Vincent, Kerry Ellis, Robert De Niro and Hannah Jane Fox caught in the flash bulbs after the premiere
Top Right: Arlene Phillips (Choreographer) appears with the 'big four' at the press conference

Ben Elton and Queen were delighted by the response at the première, with a lively audience clearly thrilled by the performances, the sharply choreographed and superbly presented tale of Galileo and Scaramouche, and the Queen songbook. Brian May and Roger Taylor took to the stage during the second and equally thunderous standing ovation, and the cast and friends then repaired to the nearby Astoria Theatre, renamed the Heartbreak Hotel for one night only, for a celebratory party.

The launch had been an unmitigated triumph, and *We Will Rock You* seemed on course to be a runaway success. But the next morning, Britain's notoriously churlish, national newspapers hit the shelves.

"We got savaged by just about every critic who came to the preview," explains Ben Elton, with a rueful smile. "It was the media at their negative worst. I thought in advance that a few critics might sneer, but

this was vitriolic, personal abuse that was nothing to do with the show. Journalists ignored the wonderful performances, the set, the production values and the technology, and they just attempted this curious mugging of me, and of Queen. *We Will Rock You* got a standing ovation on its first night, and only ten people appeared to object to the show. Sadly, they all worked as critics for the national newspapers.

"Robert De Niro phoned me, utterly baffled by the reviews, and I had to explain, 'That's just the way the press works in Britain. They hate success.' Even so, although we knew we had a fantastic show, there was a tricky time when a few people assumed that *We Will Rock You* might have to close because the reviews were so abusive. What they hadn't reckoned on was just how much normal people, as compared to journalists, would enjoy coming to the show."

Indeed. The people were about to vote with their wallets and to demonstrate their disregard for the malicious reviews. Prior to the official première, the ten preview shows had all enjoyed standing ovations.

Ben: "That meant twenty thousand people were going around London telling their friends, 'I love it.' Within a month or two, that twenty thousand had become two hundred thousand and we were able to relax.

What saved us? Simple – the amazing word of mouth, people telling their friends and family, 'You just have to see this show.'"

Despite the initial efforts of its harshest critics, *We Will Rock You* has become one of London's biggest box-office hits in recent years and the most successful rock musical since *Mamma Mia!* A modest Ben Elton is loath to hymn his own production but, when pushed, he offers an assessment of its wide appeal.

"Well, I think the show is unashamedly theatrical, in the same way that Queen were," he begins. "There is a great sense of absurdity, a lot of fun. We're not trying to be intellectually challenging, but that doesn't mean the plot isn't clever. The simplest ideas can be the hardest to come up with, and the most effective. I had some great Queen songs to work with.

"Good, popular entertainment is hard to pull off, and is often only recognized in later years. When I started out as a comedian back in the early eighties, journalists would ask me which comics I liked. They expected me to say hip icons like Lenny Bruce, but I was watching *Dad's Army* and *Morecambe & Wise* as a kid, and that's what I told them. I'd be delighted if *We Will Rock You* can carry on being a success in the same way, just because the public love it."

From a passing inspiration as Ben Elton pushed his children in a buggy through Regents Park, *We Will Rock You* has grown into a magnificent monster. Just over a year after it opened, the millionth satisfied customer passed through the Dominion Theatre's doors to delight in the preposterous, yet compelling fable of Galileo and Scaramouche. Ben Elton has lost count of the number of times that he has seen the London production – yet still regards it as a work in progress.

"One of the reasons that it has been such a success, hopefully, is that we've never stopped working on it," he ventures. "I've been in the Dominion every week for a year, and every time I watch the show, a new gag or a new way to improve on things occurs to me. Brian and Roger are exactly the same. We love this show too much ever to regard it as finished, and move on; it's always living work for us."

Anybody who has seen *We Will Rock You* more than once may have noticed that the identities of the Bohemians, dogged co-conspirators of Galileo and Scaramouche, are apt to vary. The names of Madonna, Prince, Aretha Franklin, Cliff Richard and Bob The Builder have all been incorporated and, during the summer of 2003, Charlotte Church joined their number – in a decidedly masculine form.

"Yes, I change the names of the Bohemians on a regular basis, to keep the show topical," says Ben. "I introduced Lulu a while ago, but now she is getting cut and Myleene from Hear'Say is going to make an appearance instead. It's just one of many fun, little changes that keep the show fresh."

As the Dominion show continued to entertain packed houses and its run was extended indefinitely, Ben Elton and Queen became aware that the appeal of *We Will Rock You*, like that of the band, is not limited to British shores but is truly international. On August 7, 2003, the musical opened at the Regent Theatre in Melbourne, Australia. Hands-on as ever, Ben intended to act upon the lessons he had learnt in London.

"I went to Australia for a few months to oversee the casting and to direct the production," he explains. "I've rewritten large sections of the London show for performances there. I've made sure all the topical and humorous script references work in Australia and are aimed at Australians. I'm delighted that the show has been going superbly; it opened to universal, rave reviews, with none of the chippiness of the British critics. It's been a deeply enjoyable, rewarding experience."

Since then, it has opened in Madrid, and as for the future of *We Will Rock You*, the sky, it seems, is the limit. Already set for a run in Cologne and Moscow, the show is also scheduled for both a national tour of the States and a lengthy residency in Las Vegas.

Yet while Ben Elton is thrilled by such overseas achievement, he has been most profoundly touched by the musical's massive success in his – and Queen's – home territory.

"I'm incredibly proud of how well *We Will Rock You* has done in London because I know how hard we've all worked to make it as good as it is," he reflects. "Every time I come to the Dominion, I walk through a crowd of people at the stage door and it includes teenagers, young children and pensioners. There's nothing better than watching people clap, cheer and enjoy this show that we've put together.

"Queen mean a lot to people – I knew that when I took this show on – and hopefully now *We Will Rock You* means something to them, too. I lost

Producer Phil McIntyre,
Casting Director
Pippa Ailion, Brian,
Ben and Queen's
Manager Jim Beach

Nigel Planer, who
played the part of Pop

Choreographer Arelene Phillips

Kerry Ellis and Tony Vincent

count a long time ago of the number of people who've stopped me in the theatre or in the street, or written to me, and told me that *We Will Rock You* is the best theatrical show they have ever seen in their lives. It's very gratifying and very humbling for me.

"The running costs are over a quarter-of-a-million pounds per week. It's impossible to break even, let alone make money, without charging £30 or £40 per ticket, which is an enormous investment for most people. There was no way that Queen were ever going to present anything to the public that wasn't the biggest and the best, though, because that's what Queen are all about. The fact that people who've paid that much money all stand and cheer at the end of the evening tells me that we are doing things right.

"There is something very special about *We Will Rock You*, and people have an awful lot of loyalty and love for it. I'm very proud, and I'm touched by the fact that all the lead cast members have remained unaltered since the show launched in London. They all signed up for a second year in their roles, which is very unusual in West End theatre. But they get a standing ovation from two thousand people every single night: why would they want to leave?"

It may be two years into its life, but there are no signs of Ben Elton wanting to sever his links with the West End extravaganza that is *We Will Rock You* or, indeed, with Queen themselves. There have even been rumours of a sequel. This all-singing, all-dancing production based on the music of one of rock's few truly unique, iconoclastic bands seems certain to run and run – as they say in the theatre.

"My intention was always to entertain the public and give them a great night out, and that is what I hope we have delivered," concludes Ben Elton. "Value for money is a rarity in theatre, but I think this show offers great value for money. I'm touched when I reflect that over one-quarter of the people who come to see *We Will Rock You* later come back to see it again. We get people buying tickets twice, three times, ten times. Now, I'm an entertainer – why wouldn't I be proud of that? It's a wonderful, wonderful thing."

Or, perhaps, a kind of magic... !!

By its very nature *We Will Rock You* is a constantly evolving show. For the magic to be at full strength it needs to be rooted in the time and place where it is performed. The version in this book is, with a little licence, a snap-shot of the show in April 2004 at the Dominion Theatre, London, as it celebrated its first two years of packed houses. In Spain, in Australia, in Moscow, Cologne or Las Vegas, or in the unknown future, the details of the script will forever be changing, yet wherever there is a Galileo and a Scaramouche, *We Will Rock You* will rock.

The lights fade on the auditorium, an ominous low drone shakes the ground, and magnificent, portentous, VAST music fills the air. What else could it be but INNUENDO?

The song blasts through the darkness, played by an as yet unseen live rock band, sung by an unseen chorus, and astride it all, the unmistakeable echo of the voice of Freddie Mercury.

Huge and grandiose, the music fills the air ... "'Til the end of time."

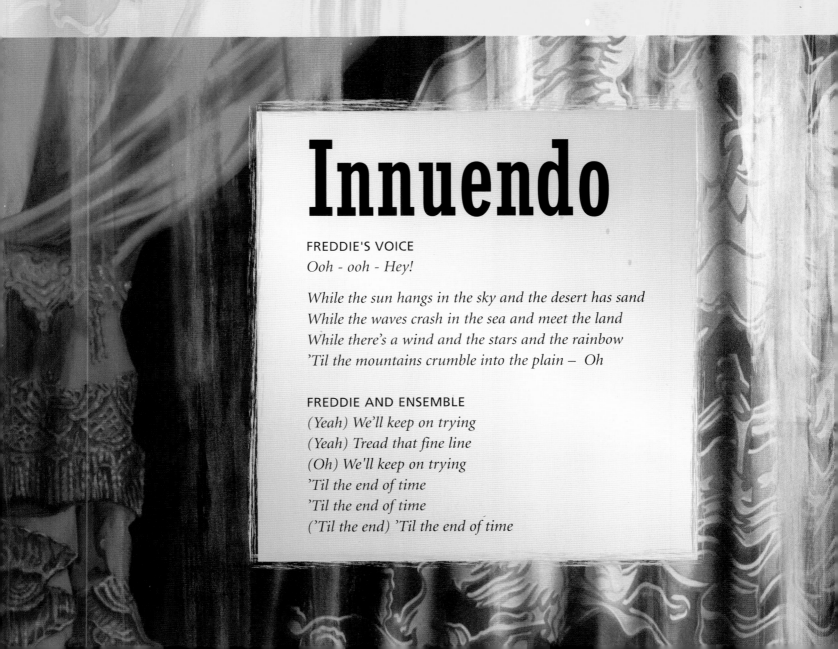

Innuendo

FREDDIE'S VOICE
Ooh - ooh - Hey!

While the sun hangs in the sky and the desert has sand
While the waves crash in the sea and meet the land
While there's a wind and the stars and the rainbow
'Til the mountains crumble into the plain – Oh

FREDDIE AND ENSEMBLE
(Yeah) We'll keep on trying
(Yeah) Tread that fine line
(Oh) We'll keep on trying
'Til the end of time
'Til the end of time
('Til the end) 'Til the end of time

Scene I

POP'S ARCHIVE
THE LASER CELL

Pop, an old hippy librarian, is furtively speaking into his dictaphone.

POP
I must make haste... for I fear my arrest
is imminent.
Stardate April 14th 2304.
Although I have yet to discover the exact date on
which the music died, it is clear to me that an
ancient entertainment phenomenon known
as "Pop Idol" played a central role.
Soon, pop stars were being created at such a rate
that they were famous for less time than it took
to play their records. Culture imploded, the
Globalsoft Corporation seized its opportunity,
and the Age of Ga Ga had dawned.

Suddenly the bright bars of a laser cell stab through the darkness. Vertical shafts of cruel light split the air, trapping Pop within. Khashoggi, the Chief of Secret Police, appears.

KHASHOGGI
Oh my. Oh my, oh my. What is this?
Do I see a little silhouetto of a spy?

POP
Bummer.

KHASHOGGI
Tell me old man, why do you concern
yourself so much with what is past?

POP
Because it is only the past that gives us hope.

KHASHOGGI
But you have read the secret histories. Surely you
have learned that there is no hope?

POP
There is always hope.

Pop's hand is caught in the laser cell.

POP (cont'd)
Hope is our birthright.

Khashoggi is losing patience, his calm explodes into
momentary rage.

KHASHOGGI
Then where is it? Where is this hope?

Pop pauses before calmly replying.

POP
Any way the wind blows.

KHASHOGGI
What do you know of the term "Living Rock"?

POP
Only that which the legend promises.
That salvation is to be found there!
At the Place of Champions! And that a
bright, bright star will show the way!

Khashoggi smiles.

KHASHOGGI
God I hate hippies!
Consign this miserable creature to The Seven
Seas of Rhye.

The Police close in on Pop, his laser cell flashes.
They place a horrifying electronic helmet on his
head. Pop grips the helmet and SCREAMS....

POP
Make love not waaaaaaaaaaaaaaar!

But he is gone. Blackout.

Scene II

VIRTUAL HIGH SCHOOL

The opening drum beat of RADIO GA GA kicks in. Now light explodes on stage to reveal massed ranks of clone-like kids. They have fixed smiles, and move with choreographed symmetrical movements. They are dressed not quite identically but in very similar clothes to each other. Happy, kooky, sexlessly sexy, youth orientated clothes, the Top Shop/Top Girl wardrobe of their era. There is something sinister about their smiles and clothes; Stepford Kids. They sing a strangely twisted version of RADIO GA GA.

Radio Ga Ga

GA GA KIDS AND THEIR TEACHERS

We sit alone and watch your light
Our only friend through teenage nights
And everything we want to get
We download from the Internet
No need to think, no need to feel
When only cyberspace is real
It makes us laugh
It makes us cry
It makes us feel like we can fly
(Globalshow)
A blueprint for our life on-line
Touch any key – the world is mine
We're lost in space but we don't care
Without your light our world's not there
Complete control – you are the power
Our lives are programmed by the hour
Globalshow (Globalshow)

All we hear is Radio Ga Ga
Video goo goo
Internet ca ca
All we hear is cyberspace Ga Ga
Marketing blah blah
Always something new?
Globalsoft – All your world loves you!

We watch our shows we watch your stars
Across our screens for hours and hours
We hardly need our eyes or ears
We just log on and dreams appear
(Globalshow)
We're not alone, we have our friends
On cyber love we can depend
So stick around 'cos we'd all miss you
We need our graphics, need our visual
Complete control, you are the power
You use our lives up by the hour
Globalshow (Globalshow)

All we hear is Radio Ga Ga
Video goo goo
Internet ca ca
All we hear is cyberspace Ga Ga
Marketing blah blah
Always something new
Globalsoft - All your world loves you
Loves you.

As the song ends the kids explode into happy clappy celebration.

Galileo enters.

Galileo is different from the young people we have just seen. He is a sullen, disaffected teen, he doesn't dress in the happy, kooky clothes the others wear, he is the James Dean of his time, a rebel without a cause, sensitive and confused. A coiled spring waiting to go boing!

TEACHER
Hey kids, school's out! It's summer time.
Get out there and have some fun!

GA GA KIDS
That is so cool! Alright!

GALILEO
Hey You!

GA GA KIDS
Yeah! What?

GALILEO
You're all clones! Ga Ga sheep!

GA GA KIDS
Talk to the hand! (click fingers)

GALILEO
Fools... Morons... Don't You understand you're all slaves?

GA GA KIDS
Whatever, loser!

The teacher is a bit hip, one of those slightly groovy teachers who are always trying to get with the kids.

TEACHER
Hey mate, come on, go celebrate!
Your life is just beginning.

GALILEO
Good! The s-sooner it begins the sooner it's over with.

Galileo has a slight stutter. We sense it is more that he can't find the words he wants to say rather than a genuine disability.

TEACHER
But you have so much potential. You could get a job with any division of Globalsoft you choose. How about music programming?

GALILEO
I don't want to programme music. I want to make music. Real music. My own music.

TEACHER (suddenly scared)
Hey! Mate, cool it.

She checks that they are not being overheard.

TEACHER (cont'd)
Now listen www/gordon@thejones's.com.

GALILEO
My name is Galileo Figaro.

TEACHER
Nobody is called Galileo Figaro. Where on Planet Mall did you come up with that?

Now Galileo's moment of strutting arrogance is over, he is scared again, scared and confused.

GALILEO
I've found it. In a dream. I have dreams you see. And I hear noises, screeching, thudding, b-banging noises. And words, words drop into my head, too many words. Help! I need somebody. Help! Not just anybody.

TEACHER
I understand. I feel your pain. But come on mate! You live in a perfect world. What more could you possibly want?

I Want To Break Free

Galileo sings I WANT TO BREAK FREE.

GALILEO

I want to break free
I want to break free
I want to break free from your lies you're so self satisfied
I don't need you
I've got to break free
God knows
God knows I want to break free

I've fallen in love
I've fallen in love for the first time
In love with a world that's for real
I've fallen in love, yeah
God knows
God knows I've fallen in love

It's strange but it's true
Hey! I know I'm diff'rent, there's so much I have to do

But I have to be sure when I walk out that door
Oh how I want to be free baby
Oh how I have to be free
Oh how I want to break free!

Guitar solo

This existence is wrong
I can't get used to livin' without livin' without
livin' without hope
It's all a lie
I don't want to live alone
But God knows
Got to make it on my own
So people can't you see
God knows I've got to
God knows I need to
God knows I WANT...
To break free

The teacher's manner has totally changed. We now realise that the teacher is a police spy.

> TEACHER
> Yes, the little freak says he hears it in his dreams.

> KHASHOGGI
> He is aware that music, other than that programmed by the Globalsoft Corporation, is illegal? The act of an Individual?

> TEACHER
> Of course, but he doesn't care.

> KHASHOGGI
> Has he ever tried to make an instrument?

> TEACHER
> Once in Technical Studies, he was caught trying to stretch plastic string across an empty lunch box.

> KHASHOGGI
> Did he – pluck it?

> TEACHER
> Yes, but he claimed he did not know why.

> KHASHOGGI
> So... an ignorant plucker! I think that I shall have to talk to this boy.

Khashoggi clicks his fingers and Galileo disappears through the floor.

A web of light descends on Galileo; it is a police laser cell. He is immobilized, frozen, surrounded by bars of light. Khashoggi and the teacher enter.

> KHASHOGGI.
> You say this boy wants to make his own music?

TEACHER
Goodbye "mate" ha ha.

KHASHOGGI
Are there any other potential Bohemians in this year's graduation groups?

TEACHER
I am sorry to have to report, Commander, that there is one other. A repulsive creature. A girl.

As the teacher speaks, there appears downstage a young girl. She is Scaramouche (she is not called this yet but we will refer to her as such to avoid complication). Scaramouche is a teenage girl who doesn't fit, like Galileo. She dresses differently from the teeny pop clones around her. She is a punk and a loner; all in black, she has swathed her body in huge dark clothes, the classic disaffected Goth teenager.

SCARAMOUCHE
I want to break free
I want to break free
I want to break free from your lies you're so
self satisfied
I don't need you
I've got to break free
God knows
God knows I want to break free

TEEN QUEEN ONE (whistles)
Check out the weirdo, girls.

TEEN QUEEN TWO
Doesn't your Mum download you anything decent to wear?

SCARAMOUCHE (defiant)
I make my own fashion statements.

TEEN QUEEN THREE
What's today's statement then? "Hallo I'm a pathetic, ugly little zero"?

TEEN QUEEN FOUR
How will you ever get with one of the boys from the Boy Zone dressed up like some sort of freak?

TEEN QUEEN FIVE
You're a disgrace to the Ga Ga Girls.

SCARAMOUCHE
I ain't no Ga Ga Girl and I'm not interested in the kind of Boys R Us derr brain zone clones you hang out with.

TEEN QUEEN ONE
You are such a sad loner.

SCARAMOUCHE (to herself)
Well you sure are right about that, bitch.

Khashoggi and his officer disappear into darkness as a nasty group of Teen Queen cheerleaders enters. They start to taunt Scaramouche.

Scaramouche and the Teen Bitches sing SOMEBODY TO LOVE, the backing vocals being delivered as brittle, girly sneers.

Somebody To Love

SCARAMOUCHE (AND TEEN QUEENS)
Can anybody find me
Somebody to love?
Each morning I get up I die a little
Can't barely stand on my feet
(Take a look at yourself in the mirror and cry)
Take a look in the mirror and cry
Lord what you're doin' to me
(Yeah yeah)
I have spent all my years in believing you
(Ooh – believing you)
But I just can't get no relief Lord
(Ooh ooh ooh Lord)
Somebody, ooh somebody
(Somebody, somebody, anybody find me)
Can anybody find me somebody to love?

TEEN QUEEN 1
Somebody to love YOU? Yeah. Right.

TEEN QUEEN 2
Hallo-o. That is SO not gonna happen.

TEEN QUEEN 3
Pull yourself together – get a virtual life!

I work hard (She works hard) ev'ry day of my life
I work 'til I ache my bones
At the end (At the end of the day)
I take home my broken heart all on my own
(Goes home on her own)
I go down on my knees and I start to pray
(Down – knees – Praise the Lord)
'Til the tears run down from my eyes Lord
Somebody – ooh somebody
Can anybody find me
Somebody to love?

(She works hard ev'ry day)
I try and I try and I try
But everybody wants to put me down
They say I'm goin' crazy
They say I got a lot of water in my brain
I got no common sense
I got nobody left to believe
Yayee yeah!

Got no feel I got no rhythm
I just keep losing my beat
(She'll just keep losing and losing)
I'm OK I'm alright
(She's alright she's alright)
No I ain't gonna face no defeat
(Yeah yeah)
I just gotta get out of this prison cell
(Ooh – this prison cell)
Someday I'm gonna be free Lord!

(Find me somebody to love)
(Find me somebody to love)
(etc.)
Oh find me find me find me...
(Somebody find me somebody to love)
Can anybody find me...
Somebody TO...
LOVE --
Somebody to love?

At the climax of the song Khashoggi emerges from the darkness, smooth and sinister.

KHASHOGGI
How very touching, young lady. But surely you understand that the company loves you? Arrest her.

SCARAMOUCHE
Globalsoft equals fascism!

Officers enter and arrest Scaramouche as the music of KILLER QUEEN kicks in ...

Scene III

THE BOARDROOM

ELECTRONIC VOICE
**Workers of Globalsoft! Junior Executives,
Senior Executives, Vice Presidents, Presidents,
Chairmen, Chairwomen, Chair-Transexuals and
Chair-Androgenous Artificially Created Life
Forms, please prepare to welcome the Chief
Executive Officer of Globalsoft Planet Wide!
www.killerqueen@globalsoft.com/theworld!**

Huge excitement as the assembled super yuppies
sing KILLER QUEEN, preparing for their monarch's
entrance.

Killer Queen

YUPPIES

She keeps Moët et Chandon
In her pretty cabinet
Let them eat cake she says
Find me on the Internet
A built-in remedy for Khrushchev and Kennedy
At any time an invitation you can't decline
Caviar and cigarettes
Well versed in etiquette
Extraordinarily nice!

She's a Killer Queen
Gunpowder, gelatine
Dynamite with a laser beam
Guaranteed to blow your mind
Anytime!
Recommended at the price
Insatiable an appetite
Wanna try?

Killer Queen appears as if by magic, in a cloud of smoke, in the middle of the boardroom table.

KILLER QUEEN AND YUPPIES

To avoid complications I never keep the same address
In conversation I e-mail like a baroness
Met a man from China, went down to Geisha Minor
But then again incidentally if you're that way inclined
(Killer, killer, she's a Killer Queen)
Perfume came virtually from Paris
(Virtually)
For cars I couldn't care less
Fastidious and precise
I'm a Killer Queen
Gunpowder, gelatine
Dynamite with a laser beam
Guaranteed to blow your mind
(Any time)

Killer Queen "conducts" the guitar soloists.

Drop of a hat I'm as willing as
Playful as a pussycat
Then momentarily out of action
Temporarily out of gas
To absolutely drive you wild
I'm out to get you...

Khashoggi appears on the video screen.

KILLER QUEEN
Commander Khashoggi!

KHASHOGGI
You screamed for me, Ma'am?

KILLER QUEEN
**The Globalsoft Board and I have been discussing
your recent security memo. We want answers.
What of the old librarian you have been
torturing? Do you take the texts which he
discovered seriously?**

KHASHOGGI
Yes, Ma'am, I'm afraid that I do.

The yuppies all gasp.

KHASHOGGI (cont'd)
**The legend clearly states that musical instruments
still exist somewhere on Planet Mall. At the Place
of Champions, hidden within the living rock.**

YUPPIE CHORUS
Oh No!

KHASHOGGI
Oh Yes!

KILLER QUEEN
But which rock and where? The whole damn planet's a rock, if you didn't know.

The yuppies laugh three times.

KILLER QUEEN (cont'd)
And what of this "shining star" that is supposed to guide us? I have had the company's finest astronomers combing the heavens for months. There is no new star.

KHASHOGGI
Not that we've spotted Ma'am, certainly.

KILLER QUEEN
Well, star or no star, I intend to blast every rock on Planet Mall to smithereens just in case. Stonehenge! Mount Rushmore! The famed Victoria Beckham Belly Button Diamond! If these grim tools of freedom do exist, I shall find them.

Yuppies clap three times.

KILLER QUEEN (cont'd)
Two more.

Yuppies clap twice.

KHASHOGGI
As always, Ma'am, you leave me limp with excitement.

KILLER QUEEN
Watch it or I'll leave you stiff with rigor mortis!

Khashoggi disappears from the screen.

KILLER QUEEN (cont'd)
And now let us return to the real business of Globalsoft. The business of the complete appropriation of the imagination of every kid on Planet Mall. Take a memo! E-mail to all consumers planet-wide, "Dear everybody in the world. Get on line you pleasure seekers! And download the Killer Queen."

Killer Queen and the company sing PLAY THE GAME. It is a highly sexy, seductive, sinister song and dance in which these super yuppies glory in their power.

Play The Game

KILLER QUEEN AND SUPER YUPPIES

Open up your mind and let me step inside
Rest your weary head and let your heart decide
It's so easy
When you know the rules
It's so easy
All you have to do is fall in love
Play the game
Ev'rybody play the game
Of love – yeah

When you're feeling down and your resistance is low
Take a cyber shopping trip and let yourself go
Give me your life
Don't play hard to get
It's a free world
All you have to do is fall in love
Play the game
Ev'rybody play the game
Of love... love

My game of love has just begun
Love runs from my head down to your toes
My love is pumping through your veins
(Play the game)
Driving you insane
(Come come come come)
Play the game, play the game
Play the game, play the game

Give me your life
Don't play hard to get
It's a free world
All you do is fall in love
Play the game
Ev'rybody play the game
Of love, of love
Oooh
Of love

At this moment of camp, semi-fascistic triumph for
Killer Queen, a corporate love fest for the super
yuppies, the Globalsoft Board Meeting is plunged
into darkness…

THE LASER CELL

Now we hear the voice of the Khashoggi, sinister and scary through the darkness.

KHASHOGGI
We found your laptop, boy. We have read the notes you keep.

Now we see Galileo alone on stage, still trapped in the cell made of laser beam bars. He snarls back into the darkness.

Khashoggi emerges from the darkness, Galileo cannot see him, but can hear him.

GALILEO
So pigs can read. You'll be flying next.

KHASHOGGI
What does "A wop bop a loo bop a lop bam boom" mean?

GALILEO
Isn't it obvious? It means "A wop bop a loo bop a lop b-bam boom."

KHASHOGGI
Do you really have a girl named Daisy who almost drives you crazy?

Now Galileo can see Khashoggi, he taunts the policeman.

GALILEO
Of course! And she knows how to love me, yes indeed, boy you don't know what she's doin' to me.

Khashoggi circles Galileo's cage.

KHASHOGGI
Then where is she? What is her e-mail address? How does she love you? How does she drive you crazy? Is she a drug pusher?

Galileo laughs; it is almost as if he wants a confrontation.

GALILEO
You're madder than I am, Pig! There is no girl named Daisy. I wish there was! I just wrote it, that's all, it appeared in my head!

KHASHOGGI
Don't play games with me, boy! I'll make you wish you'd never been born at all.

Suddenly Galileo's brittle humour leaves him and he shouts in anguish.

GALILEO
Don't you think I wish that every day!

A cop emerges to question Galileo.

FIRST COP
Where is Penny Lane?

A second cop appears.

SECOND COP
What are the Strawberry Fields?

KHASHOGGI
**"Underground, overground, Wombling free..."
Tell me boy, how do you do do do the Funky
Gibbon?**

GALILEO
I wish I knew! Oh sweet mother I wish I knew...

Galileo's confusion and anguish are painful to see.
He almost weeps. The cops exchange significant
glances.

KHASHOGGI
Galileo, do you know, what... a Bohemian is?

GALILEO
**Haven't you got it yet? I don't know what
anything is.**

KHASHOGGI
Excellent. I think we've found you just in time.

FIRST COP
The Seven Seas of Rhye, Commander?

KHASHOGGI
**Oh no, dear me not yet. Soon, yes. But first, first
I think this boy will have his uses.**

Galileo is taken away as a burst of electronic
interference fills the air. Khashoggi speaks into his
Palm Pilot.

KHASHOGGI (cont'd)
Khashoggi to Killer Queen...

POLICE HQ

The Killer Queen addresses Khashoggi from screens.

KHASHOGGI
Good news, Ma'am.

KILLER QUEEN
It had better be, I'm having my roots done.

Killer Queen addresses her hairdresser.

KILLER QUEEN (cont'd)
Get me a skinny latte... So?

KHASHOGGI
I believe that the last remaining rebels will soon
be within my clutches.

KILLER QUEEN
Then you must crush them without mercy.

KHASHOGGI
My my, Ma'am. You are an eager beaver.

KILLER QUEEN
You leave my eager beaver out of this. We were
discussing destroying the rebels.

KHASHOGGI
I advise discretion, Ma'am. The last thing we
want to do is worry the Ga Ga Kids. Particularly
now, with Summer upon us once more.

KILLER QUEEN
There are no seasons in the Virtual World,
Commander.

KHASHOGGI
Not on-line, Ma'am. But sadly the physical world
still exists. It's hot out there, hot and edgy. The
rivers are drying up, the polar ice-caps are
melting and the resistance is growing.

KILLER QUEEN
The Bohemians?

KHASHOGGI
Of course.

KILLER QUEEN (sadly)
Who are these people? What do they want?

KHASHOGGI
They want it all, Ma'am. And they want it now.
They want... their Rhapsody.

General shock at the use of this term.

KILLER QUEEN
That is a proscribed word Commander, no such
state of being exists.

KHASHOGGI
Not yet, Ma'am.

KILLER QUEEN
Not ever! The Bohemian Rhapsody is a myth! A
myth, do you hear me?! Have you not reported
that the euphoria they seek can only be
unleashed through music? Real, live, music!

KHASHOGGI
That is what they believe, Ma'am.

KILLER QUEEN
Then there will be no Rhapsody, for there are no
instruments left on Planet Mall and the kids will
never, ever make their own music again!

Under her insane laughter, we hear the menacing
sound of DEATH ON TWO LEGS, a rippling piano
growing from an echo in the darkness, only to be
swamped by dirty crunching Hitchcock-inspired
guitar chords, as the video freezes.

Killer Queen and Khashoggi disappear.

Scene VI

THE HOSPITAL

Galileo is on a hospital bed, his head is bandaged. He raises himself up. His head aches, he starts to try and discover where he is. He sees Scaramouche on another bed, her head also bandaged; she too is disorientated.

GALILEO
Hey, G-G-G-Ga Ga Girl. Who are you?

Scaramouche is, as always, hard and defensive.

SCARAMOUCHE
I ain't no Ga Ga Girl, and I don't answer questions. Who are you?

GALILEO
I'm... I don't know who I am.

SCARAMOUCHE
That must make things a bit difficult.

GALILEO (proudly)
But my name is Galileo Figaro.

SCARAMOUCHE
Cool name.

GALILEO
Thank you.

SCARAMOUCHE
I wasn't being serious. Mind if I shorten it?

GALILEO
Well, I suppose Galileo would be...

SCARAMOUCHE
So Gazza, tell me, why were you arrested?

GALILEO
Because I hear sounds in my head, words and sounds. I'm mad you see.

SCARAMOUCHE
I was arrested because they don't like the way I dress.

GALILEO
I think you dress beautifully.

SCARAMOUCHE
That's nice, except coming from a self-confessed nutter... not! What sounds do you hear?

GALILEO
I don't know.

SCARAMOUCHE
Do you know anything?

GALILEO

Yes, I know that I'm different. Which is why the clones from the Boy Zone hate me.

SCARAMOUCHE

The Ga Ga Girls hate me.

GALILEO

Do you know why they hate you?

SCARAMOUCHE

Sure. They think I'm a lesbian because I don't wear pastels.

GALILEO

They hate you because they're scared of you, because you're different – you're an individual.

SCARAMOUCHE

What do you think they did to us?

GALILEO

I don't know.

SCARAMOUCHE

Do you think they'll ever give up and leave us alone?

GALILEO

Don't you see? We're a threat.

A slow musical descent into UNDER PRESSURE begins

GALILEO (cont'd)

A virus on their hard drive, and they won't give up until they've pointed their little arrow at us...

SCARAMOUCHE

And dragged us to trash.

Under Pressure

Together they sing

GALILEO AND SCARAMOUCHE
Pressure. Pushing down on me
Pressing down on you no man asked for
Under pressure
That burns a building down
Splits a family in two
Puts people on streets
Boom bah bah bay, boom bah bah bay
De day oh De day oh
That's OK
It's the terror of knowing
What this world is about
Watching some good friends screaming
"Let me out!"
Pray tomorrow gets me higher
Pressure on people, people on streets
Day day dep – dadadabop bop – OK

Chippin' around, kick my brains around the floor
These are the days it never rains but it pours
De doh dah doh de de doh dah dah mm dah doh ba la lop
Oh
People on streets
De da dee dah day
People on streets
De da dee dah dee dah dee dah
It's the terror of knowing what this world is about
Watching some good friends screaming
"Let me out!"
Pray tomorrow gets me higher, higher, high
Pressure on people, people on streets

Turned away from it all like a blind man
Sat on a fence but it don't work
Keep coming up with love but it's so slashed and torn
Why? Why? Why?
Love, love, love, love
Insanity laughs – under pressure we're cracking

Can't we give ourselves one more chance?
Why can't we give love that one more chance?
Why can't we give love, give love, give love, give love,
Give love, give love, give love, give love, give love?
'Cos love's such an old-fashioned word
And love dares you to care for the people
On the edge of the night
And love dares you to change our way of
Caring about ourselves
This is our last chance
This is our last dance
This is ourselves
Under pressure
Under pressure
Pressure

At the end of the song they are about to embrace, but then get self-conscious realising they have nearly got carried away. They break apart in adolescent confusion.

SCARAMOUCHE
So where do we go?

Galileo is changing. Meeting Scaramouche has put some lead in his pencil; he is less tense and nervous, more strutting.

GALILEO
Out into the night! Down on the streets!
We're rebels now, 'cos Baby we were born to run.

SCARAMOUCHE
Don't call me Baby!

Galileo isn't quite grown up yet, he is immediately his old confused self.

GALILEO
Sorry, it's just a phrase I heard in my head.

SCARAMOUCHE
Yeah?

GALILEO
Yeah.

SCARAMOUCHE
Well keep it there.

Galileo and Scaramouche run off...
We hear the sound of a huge explosion.

Scene VII

KILLER QUEEN'S CONTROL ROOM

The Killer Queen and Khashoggi with a Yuppie in attendance arrive through the trap wearing hard hats. Behind them we see Stonehenge disappearing in a huge explosion.

KHASHOGGI
Goodbye Stonehenge! Well, Madam, we have now pulverised every single rock on Planet Mall and not a single Instrument of Mass Destruction has been found. The legend is a myth, or if you prefer, the myth is a legend.

KILLER QUEEN
I like it both ways.

KHASHOGGI
So I've heard, Ma'am.

KILLER QUEEN
We've won, Khashoggi. The Bohemians will never achieve their Rhapsody.

KHASHOGGI
With respect, Ma'am, the Bohemians remain dangerous, all they need is a leader. That's all it takes. One young soul rebel, one crazy kid with a dream, a guitar and a bad-arsed babe to fight for.

KILLER QUEEN
Could such a hero exist?

KHASHOGGI
Oh but he already does, Ma'am, though he doesn't know it. He does not know himself at all, but I do. I've always had a talent for spotting potential.

KILLER QUEEN
And crushing it.

KHASHOGGI
That is my job, Ma'am. And with the last dream extinguished there will be nothing left on Planet Mall but entirely untrammelled marketing and completely uncritical consumers. Put them together and what do you get?

KILLER QUEEN
Alchemy Khashoggi, pure alchemy.

As Khashoggi and the Killer Queen sing, their world is filled with computer imagery, the embodiment of their shared dreams of emotional, spiritual, and financial World Domination.

A Kind Of Magic

KILLER QUEEN, KHASHOGGI AND
YUPPIE CHORUS
One dream, one soul, one prize, one goal
One golden glance of what should be
(It's a kind of magic)
One shaft of light that shows the way
No mortal man can win the day
(It's a kind of magic)
The bell that rings inside your mind
Is challenging the doors of time
The waiting seemed eternity
The day has dawned of sanity
Is this a kind of magic?
There can be only one
This dream will last a thousand years
We will live on

This flame that burns inside of me
I'm hearing secret harmonies
(It's a kind of magic)
I ring the bell inside their minds
We're challenging the doors of time

Guitar solo, in which Killer Queen and Khashoggi
preen and pose in front of their subjects.

This is a kind of magic
There can be only one
This quest that shapes a thousand years
Will soon be – Will soon be – Will soon be
Will soon be done –
Now we are ONE

Killer Queen and Khashoggi, hand in hand,
make a grand exit.

Scene VIII

THE WASTELAND

Voices are heard from the sewers.

> BRITNEY (voice)
> I think it's clear up there Meat.

> MEAT (voice)
> Are you sure the cops have gone?

> BRITNEY (voice)
> I'm going to the surface.

> MEAT (voice)
> Be careful! I'm coming up too...

Britney and Meat emerge warily, watching out for cops.

> BRITNEY (voice)
> No! You are so stubborn.

> MEAT (voice)
> Yeahhhhhhh! But that's why you love me!

> BRITNEY
> Ok, so what we got?

> MEAT
> Well not much, it's mainly plastic and hydrocarbons. But there's a sheet of tin that we can wobble.

> BRITNEY
> Yeah.

> MEAT
> And some pebbles that make a nice rattle.

> BRITNEY
> Cool.

> MEAT
> A bottle to blow across.

BRITNEY

Alright!

MEAT

And this great wire to twang.

BRITNEY

Sweet, sweet music… If only we could find another bit of wood to bang against the one we've got.

MEAT

Yeah. Oh you naughty boy, I think I've found a big piece of wood right here.

BRITNEY

Yeah… no! Your job is to take this stuff back to The Heartbreak.

MEAT

But Brit…

BRITNEY

No! I travel alone, you know that. I can't do the things I have to do if all I'm thinking about is you.

Meat knows that she must let Brit go.

MEAT

Sometimes I wish you didn't care so much. Sometimes I wish we'd never even heard of The Vibe.

BRITNEY

You don't mean that.

MEAT

No… I suppose not, but I miss you so much, Baby. It's tougher every time you go away.

BRITNEY

I'll be back. I always come back. And one day I'll bring the Dreamer with me.

MEAT

Sometimes I think it's us that's dreaming – perhaps the music really did die.

BRITNEY

It's only sleeping, baby. It's in a deep, deep sleep. It won't be me that wakes it, but maybe one day I'll find the man who can.

Meat takes his hand.

MEAT

Oh Brit…

Swelling chords begin, heralding I WANT IT ALL.

BRITNEY

And if I could just find that lost vibe, well then we could share our love with the whole world. And you know what we'd get then don't you… We'd get it all.

I Want

Britney and Meat sing I WANT IT ALL.
They are accompanied in the chorus
by the disembodied, massed voices
of future liberated youth (off stage!)

BRITNEY AND MEAT AND THE KIDS
OF THE FUTURE (off stage)
Adventure seeker on an empty street
Just an alley creeper light on his feet
A young fighter screaming – with
no time for doubt
With the pain and anger – can't see
a way out
It ain't much I'm asking, I heard
him say
All I want is a future, move outta
my way
I want it all
I want it all
I want it all and I want it now!
I want it all
I want it all
I want it all
And I want it now

Listen all you people, come gather
round
I gotta get me a game plan, gonna
shake you to the ground
Just give me – what I know is mine

It All

*People do you hear me? Just give me
the sign
It ain't much I'm asking – if you want
the truth
Here's to the future – hear the cry of
youth!*

*I want it all
I want it all
I want it all
And I want it now
I want it all
I want it all
I want it all - and I want it
NOW !*

*Two hearts with a one-track mind
So much to do in one life time
(People do you hear me?)
Not a time for compromise and where's
and why's and living lies
So I'm livin' it all (Yes I'm livin' it all)
And I'm givin' it all (And I'm givin' it
all!)*

BRITNEY (spoken)
**Imagine it Meat, the whole world
joining in?**

MEAT (spoken)
**Thousands of people in front of
us!**

BRITNEY (spoken)
Rows and rows of them!

MEAT (spoken)
With their hands in the air!

*I want it all
I want it all
I want it all
And I want it now
I want it all
I want it all
I want it all
And I want it now*

*I want it all
Yes, I want it all
I want it all, yeah
And I want it…*

*I want it
I want it
I want it NOW*

I want it all!

They hear someone coming. Britney
grabs his bag… Quickly they hide in
the van… Galileo and Scaramouche
enter…

Their entrance reflects their growing
confidence and rebel status. They are
both very excited by their new found
freedom.

GALILEO
**I know I talk about myself a lot
but – hey – there's a lot to say…
All my life, all my life I've felt that
I have a sort of purpose, a special
destiny. That has to mean
something, surely…**

SCARAMOUCHE
**It does; that you're an arrogant,
self-important arsehole.
What special destiny?**

GALILEO
**It's to do with the stuff I dream.
The phrases, they always come
back to the same thing, I see a
great wide space and people,
people everywhere, and noise,
huge, huge noise! And then come
the words…**

SCARAMOUCHE
What words?

SCARAMOUCHE
OK, so what do you want to call me?

GALILEO (proudly)
Scaramouche.

SCARAMOUCHE
Scaramouche?... Don't you think... that's a bit...
Crap.

GALILEO
Well I dreamed some others but frankly I thought
that was the best.

SCARAMOUCHE
What were the others?

GALILEO
Long Tall Sally, Honky Tonk Woman, Lucy In the Sky
with Diamonds, or Fat Bottomed Girl.

SCARAMOUCHE
OK, I'll take Scaramouche... Scaramouche...Actually,
I kind of like it, it sounds... anarchic... almost like,
like what I think they used to call a "tune."

This comment strikes a chord with Galileo, he
remembers the words from his dream.

GALILEO
A tune, yes. Scaramouche... Scaramouche, will you
do the Fandango...?

SCARAMOUCHE
Are you trying to get into my pants?

GALILEO
No!

GALILEO
"Seek salvation in the place of living rock... A bright,
bright star will show the way... go to where the
Champions played"

SCARAMOUCHE
Sounds like bollocks to me.

GALILEO
Maybe. I think I dreamt a name for you, you know.

SCARAMOUCHE
How would you do that? You only met me today.

GALILEO
I always knew I'd meet you, that there was another
Rebel Rebel out there, another Wild Thing.

SCARAMOUCHE
Then what's doing the Fandango?

GALILEO
I think... perhaps it's... dancing.

SCARAMOUCHE
You mean Ga Ga Moves? Excuse me while I... uuuugh... puke. Globalsoft write the song and work out the steps then every kid on Planet Mall does exactly the same thing.

GALILEO
I think that maybe there was a time when dancing wasn't like that, when it was... free. Kind of individually expressive.

Again Galileo is speaking of things he only dimly understands. We hear the faintest guitar cluck and Galileo strikes a classic Freddie arm in the air pose. Then in his mind he hears the heavy Guitar Bit from BO RAP and he freaks out hippy dancing and frantically Air Guitar posturing.... Scaramouche (who, unlike the audience, has not heard the music) is not impressed.

SCARAMOUCHE
I don't think I've ever seen anything quite so embarrassing in my life.

GALILEO
It looks better when I'm holding a tennis racket.

SCARAMOUCHE
It would need to.

GALILEO
Well perhaps doing the Fandango is just about being friends.

Galileo is finally getting through Scara's shell.

SCARAMOUCHE
Friends? I... I've never had a friend.

GALILEO
What... and you with your winning ways!

SCARAMOUCHE
But I always thought I'd like one.

This is a significant moment, Scaramouche being nice.

GALILEO
So are we friends then?

SCARAMOUCHE
If you want.

GALILEO
I do! I really do!

SCARAMOUCHE
Well then, OK. We're friends.

GALILEO
This is cool.

They are drifting into a kiss... But just as Galileo is about to enfold Scara in his arms, she pulls away.

SCARAMOUCHE
As long as you promise to work on your dancing.

Meat and Britney appear from the van.

MEAT
Let's get them!

Meat advances on Scaramouche. Scaramouche responds with a karate move. Meat then pulls a flick knife out on her...

SCARAMOUCHE
Oh.

MEAT
Talk quick bitch – where did your boy friend get the words?

SCARAMOUCHE
What words?

MEAT
He calls you Scaramouche! He's read the fragments! He knows the Holy Text!

GALILEO
I don't know any Holy Text. I don't know what you're talking about!

BRITNEY
"Long Tall Sally", "Honky Tonk Woman"... The words, man, the words from the past.

MEAT
You've seen the fragments! You've been to the Heartbreak Hotel! You're a spy.

GALILEO
I said I don't know what you're talking about. I just hear things in my mind that's all!

BRITNEY
Who are you?

Galileo is again consumed with anguish.

GALILEO
I don't know! Why do people keep asking me that! I am the Walrus. This is Major Tom to Ground Control. Do you hear the drums Fernando? I am – the Dancing Queen!

Meat and Britney exchange glances – this is very strange.

BRITNEY
You... just hear these words? In your head?

GALILEO
Yes, I don't know where they come from, it drives me mad, all these phrases and sounds, stupid, useless phrases. I mean what the Hell is a Tambourine Man? What's the story morning glory? Who was The Real Slim Shady? It's torture, all I know, and I don't know why I know it, is that I really really really want to Zig-a-Zig Ah.

Britney and Meat are tense with excitement.

BRITNEY
Meat... we've found him. This dude is the one.
He's the Man.

MEAT
I say he's a spy.

BRITNEY
No, he's the Dreamer, the one we've been
waiting for, this is him.

MEAT
Test him... and his chick.

SCARAMOUCHE
"His chick"? What am I now, poultry?

GALILEO
I don't have to prove myself to you.

MEAT
Test him!

Britney and Meat check once more to see that they
are alone. Then Britney, after some preparation,
begins to sing, unaccompanied.

BRITNEY
Mama, just killed a man
Put a gun against his head
Pulled my trigger
Now he's dead.

Britney stops. There is BIG MAGIC in the air... the
lighting changes.
Britney and Meat stare hard at Galileo. This is a
strangely charged moment.... Now the light shines on
Galileo who begins to sing. He is scared and
tentative, also unaccompanied.

GALILEO
Mama, life had just begun
But now I've gone and thrown it all away...

He sings it perfectly. Britney and Meat are in awe.

BRITNEY
He knows the text, but he never read it! He's the man.

Meat turns on Galileo.

MEAT
Then what does it mean! Tell us! Who is Mama? Who's been killed? Why has it all been thrown away!

GALILEO
I don't know!

MEAT
We've been searching for the meaning all our lives.

GALILEO
I tell you I don't know! I just... hear the words, that's all.

Galileo sings again, now his voice is strong and confident. Still he is unaccompanied, and loudly proclaims..

GALILEO (cont'd)
Mama – Ooooh...

Britney and Meat hastily shut him up, but they have made their decision. This is important.

BRITNEY
You have to come with us.

MEAT
Not her. She isn't the one, we don't need her.

GALILEO
I'm not going without Scaramouche.

SCARAMOUCHE
Gazza, who says I want to go anywhere? These people could be killers.

BRITNEY
We are Baby. Killers, thrillers and Bismillahs!

MEAT
We're the resistance. The last hope.

BRITNEY
We are the Bohemians.

MEAT
And now you have a choice! Are you ready to break free?

BRITNEY
Do you want it all?

MEAT
To be a shooting star! A tiger!

BRITNEY
Defying the laws of gravity.

MEAT
Are you ready to be Champions?

SCARAMOUCHE
Nah, sounds a bit boring if you ask me.

GALILEO
What?

SCARAMOUCHE
I'm joking Gazza. Of course I want to go.

GALILEO
Alright!

The throbbing beat of HEADLONG kicks in.

BRITNEY
Then understand this, if you come with us, if you join the Bohemians, there's no way back to Ga Ga land, you'll be an outcast for ever. No longer a member of the Cons-Human Race!

SCARAMOUCHE
Sounds perfect. Let's go!

Scene IX

DESCENT INTO THE UNDERGROUND

Now as the music for HEADLONG rises triumphantly, Britney, Meat, Galileo and Scaramouche journey down into the lower depths. This is a big staging moment, and we realise through dance and special FX that they are descending into the Underworld.

Headlong

MEAT, BRITNEY, GALILEO, SCARA AND CHORUS

And you're rushin' headlong – you got a new goal
And you're rushin' headlong out of control
And you think you're so strong
But there ain't no stoppin'
And there's nothing you can do about it
Nothin' you can do, there's nothin' you can do
      about it
No there's nothin' you can
Nothin' you can
Nothin' you can
Do about it!

And you're rushin' headlong – you got a new goal
And you're rushin' headlong, out of control
And you think you're so strong
But there ain't no stoppin' and there's
Nothin' you can do about it

Hey! He used to be a man with a stick in his hand
Hoop diddy diddy – Hoop diddy do
She used to be woman with a hot dog stand
Hoop diddy diddy – Hoop diddy do
Now you got soup in the laundry bag
Now you got strings you gonna lose your rag
You're getting in a fight and it ain't so groovy
When you're screaming in the night
Get me out of this cheap "B" movie

Headlong down the highway
And you're rushin' headlong, out of control
And you think you're so strong
But there ain't no stoppin'
And you can't stop rockin'
And there's nothin' you can, nothin' you can, nothin'
you can do about it

When a red hot man meets a white hot lady
Hoop diddy diddy – Hoop diddy do
Soon the fire starts a-burnin'
Makes 'em more than half crazy
Hoop diddy diddy – Hoop diddy do
Now you start freakin' ev'rywhere you turn
You can't stop runnin' 'cos your feet got burned
It ain't no time to figure wrong from right
'Cos reason's out the window better hold on tight

You're rushin' headlong
Down the highway
And you're rushin' headlong
Out of control
You think you're so strong
But there ain't no stoppin'
And there's nothin' – nothin'
Nothin' – nothin'
Nothin' you can, nothin' you can, nothin' you can
      do about it!
HEADLONG !

Scene X

THE HEARTBREAK HOTEL

We discover Galileo, Scaramouche, Britney and Meat suddenly joined by a motley band of more weirdos and freaks who join the song at the end. They have arrived at the Heartbreak Hotel, the world of the Bohemians.

BRITNEY
Welcome to the Heartbreak Hotel.

The Heartbreak Hotel is deep beneath the city. Huge drainage and fuel pipes amongst the rocks etc. But also plastered to the walls and pipes are ancient old torn posters and bits of magazines. Classic rock memorabilia. The Bohemians are all like Britney and

Meat, weirdly dressed in a complete mix-up of rock and pop fashions. Big Macca speaks.

BIG MACCA
Who are these two, Brit?

BRITNEY
I think I've found him. The one we've been waiting for. The Dreamer.

BIG MACCA
The Dreamer? Just because he has a leather jacket doesn't make him the Wild One. He looks like a clone from the zone to me.

BRITNEY
He calls himself... Galileo.

There is general shock at this.

BIG MACCA
Galileo? Then he must have seen the texts. He's a spy.

MEAT
Which is what I said.

BIG MACCA
Kill him!

The Bohemians all rush towards Galileo, ready to attack.

BRITNEY
Anyone who tries to kill the dude has to deal with me. He hasn't seen the texts, how could he? We guard them with our lives.

Britney halts them with his arm and as his does his hand inadvertently lands on one of Prince's breasts.

PRINCE
Do ya mind! That is ma boobie!

BRITNEY
Oh sorry.

MEAT
He says he dreams the words.

BRITNEY
He calls the chick Scaramouche.

Scaramouche is getting pretty pissed off with this casual sexism.

SCARAMOUCHE
What is this "chick" business? Do I have feathers? Do I lay eggs?

BIG MACCA
Hey lady! We believe that there was a time when if a cool dude wished to refer to his red hot momma he would use the term "chick". It was a mark of respect. Second only to "bitch".

SCARAMOUCHE
Something tells me you've got that wrong.

BIG MACCA
We're getting off the point. The point is this dude is a spy.

Galileo is getting equally pissed off with being threatened.

GALILEO
Look, I don't know what you're talking about!
And I didn't ask to be brought here. I don't know
who you are or anything about your stupid texts.

BRITNEY
He just knows the stuff. It's in his head.

GALILEO
What are these "texts" anyway?

Big Macca is slowly beginning to trust Galileo.

BIG MACCA
Fragments, nothing more. Stuff that we and other Bohemians across the global shopping precinct have found.

Another Bohemian speaks up, a girl called Charlotte Church.

CHARLOTTE CHURCH
We have scraps of stuff, magazines...

SCARAMOUCHE
Magazines?

BIG MACCA
They were kind of like Web Sites but they were made of paper and you could touch them. And weird, static commercials, stuck to walls – they were called posters. We take our names from these clues from the age of rock.

ARETHA
I'm Aretha.

JACKSON FIVE
Jackson Five.

DONNY OSMOND
Donny Osmond.

BIG MACCA
And I'm Paul McCartney, they call me Sir Paul McCartney.

MEAT
And I'm Meat. You can call me Miss Loaf.

MADONNA
I'm Madonna.

PRINCE
They call me Prince.

A rather weedy youth.

CLIFF RICHARD
I'm Cliff Richard.

Another Bohemian.

CHARLOTTE CHURCH
Charlotte Frigging Church.

Another.

BOB
And I'm Bob. Bob the poet. Bob the rebel. Bob the prophet. I, am Bob the Builder.

Galileo turns to Britney – there is a connection.

SCARAMOUCHE
And who are you?

BRITNEY
And I'm the biggest, baddest, meanest, nastiest, ugliest, most raging, rapping, rock and rolling, sick, punk, heavy metal, psycho bastard that ever got get down funky. They call me Britney Spears.

GALILEO
And what is this place, this Heartbreak Hotel?

BIG MACCA
Get the man a chair please.

SCARAMOUCHE
And where do you get all this great gear? You look fantastic.

MEAT
We find it, we're scavengers.
Fancy a makeover? You're a
Bohemian now.

The girls begin to chatter excitedly
about clothes.

SCARAMOUCHE
We-e-ll

MEAT
How about some tight jeans?

SCARAMOUCHE
I hate my bum.

MEAT
A short skirt?

SCARAMOUCHE
I hate my legs.

MEAT
A cropped top?

SCARAMOUCHE
I hate my stomach... And my
hips... I quite like my arms...

MEAT
Well then let's...

SCARAMOUCHE
But not my hands...

MEAT
So, something that accentuates
your elbows?

BIG MACCA
Girls please! I am talking to The
Man here.

MEAT
Well it's better than talking out
of your bum, Paul!

BIG MACCA
"Sir Paul."

MEAT
Whatever. Go on Hen, I've got
loads of stuff back there, just
have a laugh.

SCARAMOUCHE
It's you lot that will be having
the laugh!

Scaramouche disappears behind
the tube station door. Big Macca
attempts to re-focus the Bohemians.
The mood changes.

BIG MACCA
As I was saying. This place is a
rebel base but it is also a shrine.
A shrine to all that we believe in
and a place to remember the
long dead King.

GALLILEO
What king?

The lights dim out of respect and we
hear a sombre instrumental
prologue to NO ONE BUT YOU. The
Bohemians recite their holy story
with great sadness.

BIG MACCA
Little is known about him except
that his name was Pelvis, a poor
boy from nowhere who sang
like an angel and danced like the
devil. A teenage truck driver
who broke free to become a
mighty rebel, a rebel who
spawned a thousand rebels.

PRINCE
But he was too wild, too free
and when he moved his hips the
kids felt good about themselves.
So they took him and they cut
off his hair.

BOB
Shaved his cool greasy stand-up
quiff like he was a convict.

PRINCE
And they put him in the army.

CHARLOTTE CHURCH
Then they humiliated him. The
King was forced to make foolish
movies, singing nursery rhymes
to gangs of grinning children. He
was ashamed.

MADONNA
It broke his spirit. He took

refuge in drugs and pills and –
cheeseburgers.

BOB
Like a million kids that followed.

CHARLOTTE CHURCH
The King was dead.

BIG MACCA
And many kings and heroes
died thereafter. The songs have
been lost, but their names live
on. We remember those that
died young. Buddy Holly,
Jimi Hendrix.

CHARLOTTE CHURCH
Kurt Cobain.

BOB
Janice Joplin.

PRINCE
Jim Morrison.

BOB
Bob Marley.

BIG MACCA
John Lennon.

MEAT
Freddie...

Meat sings, with the Bohemians
singing along in the choruses...

No One But You

MEAT AND THE BOHEMIANS

A hand above the water
An angel reaching for the sky
Is it raining in Heaven?
Do you want us to cry?
And everywhere the broken-hearted
On every lonely avenue
No-one could reach them
No-one but you

One by one
Only the good die young
They're only flyin' too close to the sun
And life goes on –
Without you

Another Tricky Situation
I get to drownin' in the blues
And I find myself thinkin'
Well what would do?
Yes! It was such an operation
Together paying ev'ry due
Hell you made a sensation
You found a way though

One by one
Only the good die young
They're only flyin' too close to the sun
We'll remember –
Forever

And now the party must be over
I guess we'll never understand
The sense of your leaving
Was it the way it was planned?
And so we'll grace another table
And raise our glasses one more time
There's a face at the window
And I ain't never, never sayin' goodbye... and it's

One by one
Only the good die young
They're only flying too close to the sun
Cryin' for nothing
Cryin' for no-one
No-one but you

Meat takes her bow.
Scaramouche re-enters rather
gingerly through the door.

SCARAMOUCHE
Da Dah!

Bohemians cheer and show
general appreciation.

MEAT
You look great, Hen!

SCARAMOUCHE
No I don't.

MEAT
You do, totally rock and roll!

Bohemians cheer again.

GALLILEO
That's right Scaramouche. You do look totally
rock and roll... But what is Rock 'n' Roll?

BIG MACCA
What is Rock and Roll?! What is Rock and Roll?!!

BRITNEY
Gazza Baby, Rock 'n' Roll is anything you want it
to be.

CLIFF RICHARD
It's sex.

CHARLOTTE CHURCH
It's style.

BOB
It's rebellion.

BIG MACCA
It's freedom!

GALLILEO
Yes, but what actually is it?

BIG MACCA
We don't know. All we know is that somehow
there came a day when rock and roll died. But
we have always believed in time there would
arise a man who carried the past within him.

CHARLOTTE CHURCH
A man, who could remember.

BIG MACCA
Yes thank you, Charlotte. The Fab One is talking.
Somewhere on Planet Mall there are instruments.
There must be. If Britney is right, you are the
man who will find them.

GALLILEO
Me? I don't even know what they look like!

BRITNEY
I do, look I've been working on this for months,
can't play it though. Fortunately Lulu can.

PRINCE
Lulu you're the man!

Britney produces a broom handle bass and passes it
to a Bohemian who plucks it. We hear a nasty
boinging noise.

BRITNEY

Mmmm mm. Sweet sweet noise.

Britney closes his eyes and the Bohemian twangs
the wire again, this time he hears what he wants to hear,
a beautiful bass note, much more than could really
have been produced. We start to hear something that
sounds like the bass line of CRAZY LITTLE THING
CALLED LOVE.

The Bohemians are turning into a sort of skiffle band.
They pluck and stamp and bang at what ever is at hand.

BRITNEY (cont'd)

**And then all you need is your baby, because you
see, Galileo, these days what passes for music is
created only for money, which is why it has no
soul. But when Rock 'n' Roll began you know
why they did it?**

GALILEO

Why?

BRITNEY

**They did it for their babies of course. They did it
for a crazy little thing called love.**

Crazy Little Thing Called Love

Britney and Meat lead CRAZY LITTLE THING CALLED LOVE. The company all join in, and they coax Galileo into it to, but it is clearly a love song between Britney and Meat.

BRITNEY, MEAT, GALILEO, SCARA AND THE BOHEMIANS
This thing called love, I just can't handle it
This thing called love, I must a-get round to it
I ain't ready
Crazy little thing called love
This thing called love
It cries (Like a baby) in the cradle all night
It swings, it jives
Shakes all over like a jellyfish
I kinda like it
Crazy little thing called love

There goes my baby
She knows how to rock and roll
She drives me crazy
She gives me hot and cold fever
She leaves me a cool cool sweat!

I gotta be cool, relax, get hip
Get on my tracks, take a back seat
Hitch-hike
And take a long ride on my motor bike
Until I'm ready

Crazy little thing called love

Guitar solo – the Bohemians dance.

I gotta be cool, relax
Get hip and get on my tracks
Take a back seat
Hitch-hike
And take a long ride on my motor-bike
Until I'm ready (Are you ready?)
Crazy little thing called love

This thing – called love
I just – can't handle it
This thing – called love
Just gotta get round to it
I ain't ready (Get ready!)

Crazy little thing called love
Crazy little thing called love – all right!
Oh – YEAH!

The song ends in exultant triumph – suddenly shattered as sirens wail, lights flash. There are cops everywhere. They rush on from all sides, descend from the air, appear through the floors. The Bohemians huddle together in dismay. Khashoggi enters.

KHASHOGGI
Oh yeah indeed!

Two Policemen keep Galileo and Scaramouche separated from the rest.

KHASHOGGI (cont'd)
Finally I am checking into the Heartbreak Hotel. Incarcerate the rebels!

A huge laser cage traps the Bohemians. The bars tighten, herding the shocked prisoners into a struggling, heaving mass within.

KHASHOGGI (cont'd)
And so Mr McCartney I say hello, and you say goodbye.

BRITNEY
No! You'll never take the Dreamer while I'm alive.

KHASHOGGI
You'll never escape the laser cage.

But Britney, by pure strength and endurance of pain, breaks out of the cage. Only he can do it.

BRITNEY
Galileo! Scaramouche! The future of rock lies with you!

All the Police run to seize Britney. They fight.

The riffs of OGRE BATTLE blast in. The gallant Britney single-handedly holds the cops at bay for just long enough. Momentarily Galileo is torn, but he knows that if the kids of Planet Mall are ever to be free, he and Scaramouche must run. He grabs Scaramouche's hand and they escape...

But Britney is cruelly outnumbered. It is a battle he cannot survive.

END OF ACT ONE

ACT II

Scene I

GA GA LAND

One Vision

GA GA KIDS

Hey! One plan, one goal, one mission
No heart, no soul, just one solution
One flash of light, yeah, one God, one vision
One comfort zone, one true religion
One voice, one hope
One real decision
Wowowowowowo give me one vision

Act Two opens in darkness. We hear the weird slow-mo intro, then the bass drum throb, of ONE VISION. Then, as the dirty guitar riff kicks in, the lights blast up on the surface of Planet Mall. The Ga Ga Kids in full automated glory appear. These happy clappy Stepford boys and girls sing ONE VISION.

VOICE OF FREDDIE

I had a dream when I was young
A dream of sweet illusion
A glimpse of hope and unity
And visions of one sweet union

GA GA KIDS

But a cold wind blows, and a dark rain
*   falls*
And in my heart it shows
Look what they've done to my dream!
One vision
So give us your hands
Give us your hearts
We're ready
There's only one direction
One world and one nation
On television
No hate, no fight

Just excitation
All through the night
It's a celebration
Wowowowo wowow yeah
One one one one one one one

Manic dance break.

Ahh Ahh!
One flesh, one clone, one true
*   religion*
One voice, one hope, one real
*   decision*
Give us one night – Yeah!
Give us one hope – Hey!
Just give us
One plan, one scam
One star, one night
One day – Hey Hey

Just gimme
Gimme gimme gimme
Fried Chicken!

The song ends. The applause is interrupted by Police sirens and search lights. We hear an electronic announcement.

POLICE MEGAPHONE
Rebel alert, rebel alert.

The Ga Ga Kids exit with urgency.

Scene II

WRECKED VAN

Galileo and Scaramouche appear through the grills, exhausted and alone, lost in the Underworld.

GALILEO
How did Khashoggi find the Heartbreak Hotel?

SCARAMOUCHE
He must have some way of tracking us.

GALILEO
The hospital! When they operated on our heads!

Galileo takes hold of Scaramouche's head, and gently explores it with his fingers.

GALILEO (cont'd)
I think... I think I've found something.

Scaramouche gets a shard of glass from the van.

SCARAMOUCHE
Cut it out.

GALILEO
What?!

SCARAMOUCHE
Gazza, if there are bugs in our heads then the cops will run us down in hours. Cut it out!

Reluctantly Galileo takes the shard of glass and as gently as he can cuts into Scaramouche's hair line. Scaramouche gasps in pain and there is blood, but he removes a flashing device which "beeps" gently and writhes like a snake – apparently some disgusting real living bug has been implanted.

GALILEO
He had us from the start. He's heard everything...

SCARAMOUCHE
Hello pervert! Short sentence... the second word is "off"!

GALILEO
OK now me.

She takes the glass and cuts into Galileo's head. She too produces a flashing bug.

GALILEO (cont'd)
Quick, crush them.

SCARAMOUCHE
What? A couple of state of the art micro transceivers? No way, I'll just activate the maximum negativity spectrum.

GALILEO
What?

SCARAMOUCHE
Turn them off.

GALILEO
We're all that's left now, Scaramouche, you know that don't you? The Bohemians are finished. The Heartbreak Hotel destroyed. Only we escaped.

SCARAMOUCHE
Britney Spears died to save us. To save you.

GALILEO
And he must not have died in vain. It's up to us

now. We're part of the Underworld,
Scaramouche. You and me, cast adrift. There's no
going back, not now, not ever.

SCARAMOUCHE
We never belonged anyway. Did you notice, you
lost your stutter?

GALILEO
I feel different.

SCARAMOUCHE
We're both different... For the first time in my
life I don't hate myself.

GALILEO
And I don't want to die.., I've found something
to live for.

SCARAMOUCHE
The Dream?

GALILEO
You.

The music for WHO WANTS TO LIVE FOREVER
begins. For a moment they look into each other's
eyes.

GALILEO (cont'd)
But we will be caught in the end. You know that
don't you?

SCARAMOUCHE
Yes. I know, and probably killed.

GALILEO
I love you Scaramouche.

SCARAMOUCHE
I love you too Gazz.

GALILEO
Do you think maybe just once you could use my
whole name?

SCARAMOUCHE
I love you too, Gazza Fizza.

She touches him tenderly.

GALILEO
Well if you love me, then dying doesn't matter
very much at all, does it?

They sing WHO WANTS TO LIVE FOREVER
tentatively, tenderly, sure that their life together is
doomed, yet edging ever closer, for truly they are
falling love.

Who Wants To Live Forever

SCARAMOUCHE AND GALILEO

There's no time for us – there's no place for us
What is this thing that builds our dreams
Yet slips away from us?
Who wants to live forever?
Who wants to live forever? – Ooh
There's no chance for us – it's all decided for us
This world has only one sweet moment set
aside for us

Who wants to live forever?
Who wants to live forever? – Ooh...

Who dares to love forever?
Oh – when love must die

Guitar solo

But touch my tears with your lips
Touch my world with your finger tips
And we can have forever – and we can love forever
Forever is our today

Who wants to live forever?
Who wants to live forever?
Forever is ours
Who waits forever anyway?

Now at last they embrace, and their embrace melts
into love-making.

The lights fade...

Scene III

LASER CAGES

Now we hear the sinister and urgent throb of FLASH intruding on the darkness. The lights come up to reveal a terrible sight. The surviving Bohemians, Big Macca, Madonna, Aretha, Meat, etc, are being held captive by Khashoggi's doctors, each of whom is armed with a brain-washing helmet. Khashoggi hovers above them in a "Ming The Merciless"-style pod.

KHASHOGGI
What do you know of the phrase "Living Rock"? Where is The Place of the Champions?

BIG MACCA
They are freedom words, Pig... Words the Dreamer used. We don't know what they mean.

The prisoners are all connected to computer screens revealing the inner workings of their brains and bodies.   One of the doctors is studying his captive's screen.

DOCTOR ONE
He tells the truth, Commander Khashoggi. I have applied a search programme to his brain functions and find no evidence of deceit.

KHASHOGGI
Pity... Hurt him anyway.

The doctor hits a button and a vast bolt of power is shot through Big Macca's screaming body. It is punctuated by a massed cry... FLASH! – AH AH!

Flash

POLICE AND BOHEMIANS
Flash! Ah-Ah!
Flash! Ah-Ah!
Flash! Ah-Ah!

KHASHOGGI
I would rather you did not call me "Pig".

Madonna defies Khashoggi.

MADONNA
Pig's too good for you!

KHASHOGGI
Hurt her also.

Again the hook FLASH AH-AH! blasts out as
Madonna is terrifyingly zapped.

KHASHOGGI (cont'd)
In fact, hurt them all!

One more time the hook FLASH AH AH! blasts out as
all the Bohemians are zapped. Now the slow refrain
of FLASH becomes the underscore.

KHASHOGGI (cont'd)
For what it's worth, your "Dreamer"
knows no more about the place of
Living Rock than you or I do. He is a
poor idiot, parroting phrases which he
does not understand. Still, he led me to
you, and for that I am grateful.

PRINCE
Are you going to kill us?

KHASHOGGI
Please, Mr Prince? Globalsoft is not
some Medieval Inquisition. We are
merely going to kill your souls. Empty
your brains of such absurd notions as
real music and individual thought.

BIG MACCA
You're sending us to Euro Disney?

KHASHOGGI
Funny! No, I was thinking more of The Seven Seas of
Rhye. Prepare the helmets!

MEAT
Dreamer, follow us. Bohemians, give him your power.
Make your last thoughts "The Dream".

KHASHOGGI
Goodnight, Miss Loaf!

ALL
NO!!!!

The piano riff of SEVEN SEAS OF RHYE strikes up and the
doctors apply the brain-washing helmets. The Bohemians
are horrified and try to fight. They struggle desperately
but to no avail, gradually being subdued. Khashoggi and
the doctors sing SEVEN SEAS OF RHYE.

Seven Seas Of Rhye

**KHASHOGGI AND DOCTORS
AND BOHEMIANS**

Fear me you lords and lady preachers
I descend upon your Earth from the skies
I command your very souls you unbelievers
Bring before me what is mine
The Seven Seas of Rhye
Can you hear me you peers and privy councillors
I stand before you naked to the eyes
I will destroy any man who dares abuse my trust
I swear that you'll be mine
The Seven Seas of Rhye

Sister – I live and lie for you
Mister – do and I'll die
You are mine, I possess you
Belong to you forever
(Forever ever ever)

Guitar solos

Storm the master marathon, I'll fly through
By flash and thunder fire and I'll survive
(I'll survive, I'll survive)
Then I'll defy the laws of nature and come out
*   alive*
Then I'll get you
Be gone with you, you shod and shady senators
Give out the good, leave out the bad evil cries
I challenge the mighty Titan and his troubadours
And with a smile
I'll take you to the Seven Seas of Rhye!

EX-BOHEMIANS

Oh I do like to be beside the seaside
I do like to be beside the sea...

Then they disappear.

WRECKED VAN

We are back in the lower depths with Galileo and Scaramouche. Galileo is asleep, Scara is awake, tinkering with something.

Galileo awakes with a start.

GALILEO
The Seven Seas of Rhye!

SCARAMOUCHE (very chirpy)
Well good morning Gazza! Or perhaps I should use your full name, Shagileo Gigolo!

GALILEO
I've had this dream and...Shagileo Gigolo?

(pleased) You really think so?

SCARAMOUCHE
Oh yes.

She leans across to embrace him, and he almost succumbs.

GALILEO
No, Scaramouche, we don't have time! The Seven Seas of Rhye, I've been dreaming about Paul McCartney and the others. I dreamt that there were cops and there were cages made of lasers and...

SCARAMOUCHE
Gazza, believe me there is nothing, and I mean nothing, more boring than people wanting to describe their dreams to you.

GALILEO
No but really...

SCARAMOUCHE
Trust me on this, it kills relationships stone dead. The day one partner wakes up and starts saying "It was amazing, there was this rabbit in a

bowler hat cooking an omelette..." that's when love dies.

GALILEO
Scaramouche, I'm sure of it. The Bohemians are heading across the Seven Seas of Rhye.

SCARAMOUCHE
I know.

GALILEO
I think it's somewhere in the Euro precinct of Planet Mall – there's water, lots of water... What?

SCARAMOUCHE
I know about the Seven Seas of Rhye. They're not seas at all, but rivers, rivers that supply a lake. They used to call it Lake Geneva. The Spirit of Rock is very strong there. It's where they put the misfits, the rebels.

GALILEO
But this is incredible, Scaramouche! We've had the same dream! It's like we're soul-mates, split aparts, kindred spirits...

SCARAMOUCHE
Gaz, I didn't have any dream, I've just reversed the polarity on one of Khashoggi's micro transceivers. I've been monitoring Police Headquarters.

GALILEO
Wow, you certainly know how to make a guy feel inadequate.

SCARAMOUCHE
Oh bless! Let me make it up to you.

Once more she leans across.

GALILEO
No! I have to go to the Seven Seas.

SCARAMOUCHE
Pretty dangerous, the cops are bound to be still after us. I say we hide out here on this mattress ... for a few days... and while we're here...

GALILEO
No Scara, I still haven't found what I'm looking for. I can't get no satisfaction. You don't stop till you get enough... Aaaah (Angry and confused) Ga... doo doo doo, push pineapple shake the tree.

SCARAMOUCHE
Pardon?

GALILEO
I'm sorry, I don't know where that last bit came from. Look, I'm going, Scaramouche, but I shall come back and...

SCARAMOUCHE
Hang on, what do you mean? There'll be cops all over the place. I should go, not you.

GALILEO
Forget it, Scaramouche, this is my fight!

SCARAMOUCHE
Excuse me? How do you work that out?

GALILEO
Because I'm the Man! Britney Spears said so.

SCARAMOUCHE

Exactly, which is why it's stupid for you to risk your life. I'm dispensable. You stay here.

GALILEO

Oh yeah, like I'm really going to let my chick go fight my battles for me!

SCARAMOUCHE

"Let your chick?!" Excuse me, but at what point in our relationship did you actually take the arse-hole pill?

GALILEO

Oh for God's sake, Scaramouche, does everything always have to be a fight with you? I thought you said you'd mellowed out?

SCARAMOUCHE

Well I haven't!

GALILEO

Well you know it's really starting to irritate me.

SCARAMOUCHE

Oh no! My heart just broke.

GALILEO

Look! You're my girlfriend and I want to protect you.

SCARAMOUCHE

You think just because you got your leg over, you own me or something?

GALILEO

Oh you are such a pain with this constant female assertion thing!

SCARAMOUCHE

Fine! At least we now know where we stand.

GALILEO

Yes we do!

SCARAMOUCHE

Which is not together!

GALILEO

If you say so!

SCARAMOUCHE

Right! From now on our relationship is purely professional. We have a job to do and we'll do it, that's all.

GALILEO

Suits me. But I'm going to the Seven Seas.

SCARAMOUCHE

So am I, but if when you get there you get caught, and the Dream is lost and the kids are enslaved till the end of time, you're going to feel a bit bloody stupid, that's all.

They storm off in different directions, furious.

KILLER QUEEN'S PAD

Fat Bottomed Girls

Killer Queen is discovered in her boudoir with a veritable army of scantily-clad chamberpersons. She sings FAT BOTTOMED GIRLS.

KILLER QUEEN WITH YUPPIES (AND OFFSTAGE CHORUS)

Oh you gonna take me home tonight
Oh down beside that red fire light
Oh you gonna let it all hang out
Fat bottomed girls you make the rockin' world
*   go round*

Hey! I was just a skinny lass
Known for sitting on my ass
But I knew life before I left my nursery – Huh!

Left alone with big fat Fanny
She was such a naughty nanny
Heap big woman you made a bad girl out of me!

Oh you gonna take me home tonight
Oh down beside that red fire light
Oh you gonna give it all you got
Fat bottomed girl you make the rockin' world
*   go round! – Yeah!*
Fat bottomed girl you make the rockin' world go
Round! Round! Round!

Khashoggi rushes on. He seems a little nervy.

KHASHOGGI
Ma'am, I bring splendid news!

Killer Queen clicks her fingers to dismiss the yuppies upstage.

KHASHOGGI (cont'd)
My officers have been successful in breaking up the Bohemian stronghold! The Heartbreak Hotel is destroyed!!!

KILLER QUEEN
Khashoggi this is wonderful! The Resistance is vanquished! We've won!

KHASHOGGI
Uhm yes, Ma'am, except if I might contin...

Don't Stop Me Now

But the Killer Queen is too happy to listen and interrupts Khashoggi with the opening of DON'T STOP ME NOW.

KILLER QUEEN
Tonight I'm gonna have myself a real good time

KHASHOGGI
Yes Ma'am, if I could just...

KILLER QUEEN
I feel ali - hi- hi- ive!

KHASHOGGI
Ma'am it's just that....

KILLER QUEEN
And the world, turning inside out
Floating around in ecstasy
So...

KHASHOGGI
Ma'am

KILLER QUEEN
Don't stop me now...

KHASHOGGI
Ma'am

KILLER QUEEN
Don't stop me
'Cos I'm having a good time, having a good time
I'm a shooting star leaping through the sky
Like a tiger defying the laws of gravity...

KHASHOGGI
MADAM!

KILLER QUEEN
I'm a racing car passing by
Like Lady Godiva I'm gonna...

KHASHOGGI
MADAAAAM!!!

The music and Killer Queen's celebration come to a grinding halt.

KILLER QUEEN
Leave!

The yuppies exit.

KASHOGGI
I'm afraid that you did not let me finish. We broke
up the Heartbreak Hotel but I fear that the
Dreamer and his bad-arsed babe slipped through
our clutches. However, I don't see this as a...

KILLER QUEEN
You lost them!

KHASHOGGI
Well lost them only in the sense of... don't know
where they are.

KILLER QUEEN
I am sick of excuses Commander Khashoggi! And I
am also sick of you.

KHASHOGGI
Ma'am?

KILLER QUEEN
With your weary, sneery, posy, schmozey "Look at
me I'm wearing my sunglasses indoors" crap.

Khashoggi whips off his shades.

KILLER QUEEN (cont'd)
Oiling around the place, your snooty little booty in
your Armani suitey.

KHASHOGGI
Actually, Ma'am, it's M&S. They've really rather
raised their game lately, don't you think?

KILLER QUEEN
Need I remind you that besides being Business
Woman of the Year, I am also Dynamite with a Laser
Beam.

KHASHOGGI (gently panicking)
No one admires you more than I do Ma'am. Your
gentle manner, your quiet unassuming sense of style.
Your generous, forgiving nature...

KILLER QUEEN
You know what happens to people who disappoint
me. I think it's time to blow your mind.

Another One Bites The Dust

Killer Queen sings ANOTHER ONE BITES THE DUST. It is a very cool, sinister killing song. Delivering it, Killer Queen continually taunts and threatens Khashoggi, prior to delivering him to his punishment. All the sycophantic yuppies cower before her, and fall to the ground at her command, as if they were part of some bizarre video game. They are.

KILLER QUEENl

*Hey! Killer Queen walks warily
down the street
With the brim pulled way down
low
Ain't no sound but the sound of
her feet
Machine guns ready to go
Are you ready? Hey!
Are you ready for this?
Are you hanging on the edge of
your seat
Out of the doorway the bullets rip
To the sound of the beat – yeah*

*Another one bites the dust
Another one bites the dust
And another gone and another gone
Another one bites the dust
Hey – I'm gonna get you too
Another one bites the dust*

*How do you think I'm gonna get
along
Without you when you're gone
I took you for ev'rything that you
had
And kicked you out on your own
Are you happy? Are you satisfied?
How long can you stand the heat?
Out of the doorway the bullets rip
To the sound of the beat. Look out*

*Another one bites the dust
Another one bites the dust
And another one gone and another
one gone
Another one bites the dust
Hey – I'm gonna get you too
Another one bites the dust ...
Hey ! Oh Shoot!*

*There are plenty of ways that you
can hurt a man
And bring him to the ground
You can beat him you can cheat
him
You can treat him bad and leave
him when he's down yeah
But I'm ready, yes I'm ready for you
I'm standing on my own two feet
Out of the doorway the bullets rip
Repeating to the sound of the beat –
yeah!*

*Another one bites the dust
Another one bites the dust
And another one gone and another
one gone
And another one bites the dust
Hey I'm gonna get you too
Another one bites the dust*

*Another one bites the dust
Another one bites the dust
Oh another one bites the dust
Another one bites the dust
Yeah yeah yeah yeah Ow!*

Khashoggi is ruined, humiliated and finally zapped, dispatched with one of his own brain-washing helmets.

Scene VI

OUT ON THE ROAD

Scara and Galileo are out on the run. Clearly they have been bitching for 200 miles.

SCARAMOUCHE
Oi! Oi! Slow down will you!

GALILEO
No! You keep up!

SCARAMOUCHE
I've got shorter legs than you!

GALILEO
Don't worry, your mouth makes up for them.

SCARAMOUCHE
You didn't have any objections to it last night.

GALILEO
That is below the belt!

SCARAMOUCHE
Which seems to be all you think women are good for!

GALILEO
Hey – we're not on some feminist awareness course here, Babe, it's a battle as big as the planet!

SCARAMOUCHE
As big as your ego more like!

GALILEO
Me, egotistical? Let's get one thing straight here. You're a girl. You're slower than me, weaker than me...

SCARAMOUCHE
Cleverer than you...

GALILEO
What? Just because you managed to reverse
the polarity on a couple of microtransceivers?

SCARAMOUCHE
Yes.

GALILEO
My intelligence is abstract! I have the mind
of an artist.

SCARAMOUCHE
A piss-artist more like!

GALILEO
A rock artist! And I have a world to save,
so if you're going to hold me up then...

SCARAMOUCHE
Hold you up?! Listen mate. We're in this
together, and despite the fact that you're
emotionally immature, scared of commitment
AND you kept your socks on, I'm staying!

GALILEO
Suit yourself!

SCARAMOUCHE
Don't worry. I will!

Hammer To Fall

Together they sing an edgy, spirited HAMMER
TO FALL.

After the crashing opening instrumental
opening blasts in, together they sing and
scream an edgy, angry HAMMER TO FALL to
each other. The song has become a fierce
domestic shoot-out, a venting of both their
frustrations.

GALILEO
Hey!

SCARAMOUCHE (parodying)
Hey!

GALILEO
Yeah!

SCARAMOUCHE
Yeah!

GALILEO AND SCARAMOUCHE
Here we stand or here we fall
History won't care at all
Wake the dead – fight the fight
Lady Mercy won't be home tonight

You don't waste no time at all
Don't hear the bell but you answer the call
It comes to you as to us all
We're just waiting for the hammer to fall

Hey!   Hey!

Yeah!   Yeah! The hammer to fall

Oh ev'ry night and ev'ry day
A little piece of you is falling away
But lift your face the Western way Babe
Build you muscles as you body decays
Toe your line and play their game
Let the anaesthetic cover it all
'Til one day they call your name
You'll know it's time for the hammer to fall
Yeah!
The hammer to fall

Rich or poor
Or famous for your truth
It's all the same
Oh no, oh no
Lock your door but rain is pouring
Through your window pane
Oh no
Baby now your struggle's all in vain

What the hell we fighting for
Just surrender and it won't hurt at all
You've just got time to say your prayers
While you're waiting for the hammer to
Hammer to fall

Ay – oh ! Ay – oh !
The hammer to fall

Ooh yeah! Ooh yeah!
The hammer to fall
Hey! The hammer to, hammer to, hammer to fall

GALILEO
Give it to me one more time!

SCARAMOUCHE (spoken)
In your dreams, mate!!!

THE SEVEN SEAS DRINKING CLUB

We discover Pop, who was interrogated in the first scene. He is a barman. He moves crates of beer around, polishes glasses and, mournfully and wistfully, sings THESE ARE THE DAYS OF OUR LIVES.

These Are The Days Of Our Lives

POP AND BRAIN-WASHED BAR PATRONS

Sometimes I get to thinking
I was back in the old days, long ago
When we were kids when we were young
Things seemed so perfect, you know?
The days were endless, we were crazy, we were young
The sun was always shining, we just lived for fun
Sometimes it seems like lately I just don't know
The rest of my life's been just a show

Those were the days of our lives
The bad things in life were so few
Those days are all gone now but one thing remains
When I look, I find no change

You can't turn back the clock
You can't turn back the tide
Ain't that a shame?
I'd like to go back one time on roller-coaster ride
When life was just a game
No use in sitting and a-thinking on what you did
When you can lay back and enjoy it through the kids
Sometimes it seems like lately
I just don't know
Better sit back and go with the flow – 'cos

These are the days of our lives
They're flown in the swiftness of time
These days are all gone now but one thing remains
When I look and I find
HOPE still survives
Oh yeah!

The bar is surrounded by natural beauty, there are mountains and through the great windows of the bar can be seen a vast lake. We notice that Big Macca, Aretha and Madonna etc are sitting almost motionless at tables. They seem lost and empty.

At the end of the song Galileo and Scaramouche enter. They see their old friends and are delighted.

GALILEO
Big Macca! Meatloaf! You guys are all here!
It's so good to see you!

SCARAMOUCHE
How did you escape?

GALILEO
This is fantastic. The Bohemians are back!
The fight is on!

But their old friends are now brain-fried zombies.

BIG MACCA
Do I know you, kid?

Pop interjects from behind the bar.

POP
Your friends aren't there, dude. Their bodies are,
but their spirits are gone. They've been
processed, man.

Galileo and Scaramouche go to the bar.

GALILEO
What do you mean?

POP
This is where they all come, the guys and chicks who tried to break on through to the other side and failed. They come to drown themselves in the Seven Seas of Rhye – Rye Whiskey, man, the last comfort of those who have rocked.

Pop puts a bottle of Jack on the counter.

SCARAMOUCHE
Why do they come here?

POP
You mean apart from in order to get permanently pissed?

SCARAMOUCHE
Yes.

POP
There's something about this place, It's like there's a spirit here. Long ago, before global warming, the lake was much smaller. Who knows, maybe there's something beneath the water. Something those washed-out mothers need to be close to.

SCARAMOUCHE
So who are you?

POP
I was a librarian, Astral Babe. At the place where the Secret History is kept. I got a little too interested in the stuff I was reading.

SCARAMOUCHE
They processed you?

POP
They tried, but I guess I knew too much, they couldn't zap it all. I may be pretty screwed up but I'm still the most together dude at the Seven Seas. That's why I'm the barman.

SCARAMOUCHE
So you remember something of what you read. Of the secret history?

POP
I remember one story. A legend so strong and powerful that they could not wipe it from my brain. Would you like to hear it?

SCARAMOUCHE
No, I thought we'd just have a quick drink and bugger off!

POP
Ouch! Balls broken!

GALILEO
Of course we want to hear it, Mr, uhm...

POP
Pop, they call me Pop.

GALILEO
Perhaps you could...

The lights dim in the bar except on Pop, Galileo and Scaramouche at the bar.

POP

Well it seems that long ago, in the first decade of the Twenty-First Century, there were those who foresaw the nightmare that was to come. This was at the very beginning of music homogenisation, a time of boy bands and girl bands ... and boy and girl bands ... and girl bands with a couple of boys that looked like girls... They called them bands but they weren't bands at all. They were just pretty-pretty dancers with multi- tracked voices.

GALILEO

It's been that way ever since.

POP

Exactly. A three hundred year bum vibe.

GALILEO

It all sounds so plausible, but how can you be so sure?

POP

Because it was foretold. Take a look at this.

Pop crosses behind the bar and produces a video tape.

GALLILEO

Wow! What is it?

POP

It's a "Vy-dayo"... a "VY-DAYO TARP". An ancient scroll of holy text.

BOHEMIANS

Ohhhhh...

POP

They all want it you know. They all want the "VY-DAYO TARP", but I've got it... it's mine... it's my precious. It's a message from the past. A warning laid down for us in antiquity. I stole it on the day I was captured and through ten long years of Hell in a laser cell I kept it hidden... secreted... out of sight... wedged deep within the murky cleft of my sweaty...

SCARAMOUCHE

Too much information Pop! Just tell us what it is.

POP

Watch this oh ye seekers after truth... I'll just slip the VY-DAYO in the teelee... listen to precious, and learn.

This is a BIG MOMENT. Pop inserts the tape and presses play. We hear the famous opening moments from

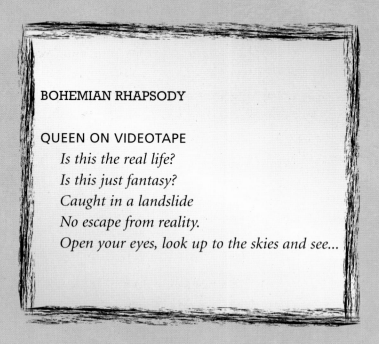

BOHEMIAN RHAPSODY

QUEEN ON VIDEOTAPE
> *Is this the real life?*
> *Is this just fantasy?*
> *Caught in a landslide*
> *No escape from reality.*
> *Open your eyes, look up to the skies and see...*

Then silence. Pop presses the stop button.

POP

That's all there is. The rest unfortunately is an episode of something called "The Young Ones".

GALLILEO

But that was so beautiful. What does it mean?

POP

Isn't it obvious? "Is this the real life? Is this just fantasy?"

SCARAMOUCHE

Yeah?

POP

Cyber-Space! The scroll speaks of a soulless, virtual world where the kids would be "caught in a landslide" of Computer Recorded Anodyne Pop... C-R-A-P!

GALILEO

Crap!

POP

Exactly! The scroll predicts a time when "Crap" would dominate the charts. The text begged the kids to "Open their eyes..."

GALILEO
"Look up to the skies..."

POP
"And see."

SCARAMOUCHE
Wow! So you really think that's what it meant?
I thought it sounded like a load of pretentious
old bollocks.

POP
No way, crazy lady! These are the words of truth.
If only we knew the rest of the text.

GALILEO
I think I know some of it. Tell me, old wise one,
what does "Bismillah. We will not let you go – let
me go. No no no no no. Mama mia mama mia,
mama mia let me go. Beelzebub has a devil put
aside for me" mean?

Pop thinks for a moment.

POP
Actually I think that bit probably WAS a load of
pretentious old bollocks.

GALILEO
But who created the scroll? Who were these
geniuses, these visionary prophets?

POP
Warriors, Titans! Members of a rock freedom
fighter collective known as... Queen! And having
issued their warning, and having incidentally
spent nine weeks at Number One with it, despite
what were quite frankly some rather dodgy
stage outfits, Queen decided to fight back!...

Pop pulls chair away from a Bohemian who falls over.

POP (cont'd)
Alright Cliff?

CLIFF RICHARD
Just a bit pissed pop.

POP
Don't worry about Cliff Richard. He's
indestructible! In order to protect the future of
Rock'n'Roll, Queen decided to bury their finest
instruments against a time when there would
be none!

GALILEO
You mean real instruments still exist?
Somewhere, waiting to be found!

POP
Yes. But for three hundred years they have lain
hidden. Queen wove deep and terrible spells to
protect the precious weapons of freedom from
abuse by those not worthy of playing them. Even
at the beginning of the Dark Age of
Globalization, Queen knew that when the time
was right, a hero would be found and the
instruments would reappear. Perhaps you are
that man, Man.

SCARAMOUCHE
What happened to Queen?

POP
The first of their number died young. Too wild,
too beautiful for this world. The other three
rocked on into the new century, pausing only to
create a smash hit musical based on their
greatest hits, but during Globalsoft's first battles

for the soul of the Planet all three were captured and secretly killed... It is said that the hairiest of the gang, a man named Bri-an, was granted a final wish before execution. He asked to be allowed to play just one last guitar solo... And so was able to delay his death by three and a half days. Where are the instruments, Galileo Figaro?

GALILEO
Me? How would I know, man? A couple of weeks ago I was virtually a Virtual High School drop out. Why would the Rock Gods tell me the answer?

Suddenly we hear vast rumbling sounds... It is the noise of water, millions of gallons of rushing water... The whole of the Seven Seas is shaking.

SCARAMOUCHE
What's going on?

POP
Don't freak out, Sweet Lady, they're just draining the lake, they steal our water all the time now, it's almost down to its original level...

Galileo has seen something...

GALILEO
Look... Look! What is that, emerging from the waters? A man!

SCARAMOUCHE
A statue.

GALILEO
A hero made from bronze and rock.

Everyone turns to look. Even the zombies know that something extraordinary is happening... As an eerie yet glorious underscore of WE ARE THE CHAMPIONS plays, upstage, there is a transformation and now there is a dazzling view across the gorgeous lake. In the middle, half submerged but slowly being revealed, bathed in light, standing heroic and proud, it is...

THE FREDDIE STATUE!!

SCARAMOUCHE
Who is it, who does it represent?

POP
I know this man... I saw many images in the Secret History... He is one of the freedom fighters of Queen!... the first to die... The greatest, brightest star of his time!

Now the penny is dropping for Scaramouche.

SCARAMOUCHE
Star! Bright star! Gazza, your dream! The bright bright star that will show the way. The star isn't a star in the sky at all – it's a rock star!!

POP
Freaky!

GALILEO
But what? What is he showing us?

SCARAMOUCHE
The way! It must be, the way to the place of Living Rock! Living Rock isn't granite and stone at all, it's music!

GALILEO

But Queen buried the instruments there. How can they be buried in music?

POP

The place of living rock, Man, live rock and roll music! He's looking towards it, Dude! The star is facing North! Well, North and a little bit West actually. To the place he once ruled! The place where people came together, to play and to be together...

GALILEO

The place where the champions played?

POP

Yes, the Place of Champions! The old arena!... I'm sure of it! The machine may have destroyed the stands and the towers, but they could never destroy the vibe of what they once called... Wembley Stadium!

SCARAMOUCHE

Galileo we have to move quickly. Now that the star has shown us the way, it can guide the Police there too, there's no time to lose.

POP

I'll come with you, I can show you how to get there.

GALILEO

But we need transport! We need wheels!

The opening bars of BICYCLE RACE kick in.

BOHEMIANS
Bicycle! Bicycle! Bicycle!

SCARAMOUCHE

Bugger that, we have to save rock 'n' roll! We can't turn up on a bike!

POP
It's very eco.

SCARAMOUCHE
But not very cool.

POP
You're right, Crazy Lady. We'll take my Harley! Rock's transport of choice. Not as fast, clean or efficient as a Japanese bike, but it sounds humungus!

Pop's Harley appears on the stage trap.

POP (cont'd)
You get on behind me, Baby. Nice. It's been years since I've felt the soft warm thighs of a rebel chick wrapped round my skinny white arse.

SCARAMOUCHE
Forget it, I'll go in front.

POP
Well all right but don't blame me if I push the bone.

SCARAMOUCHE
I felt that... Gazza, get on behind me. And don't get any fresh ideas.

GALILEO
It's time. Time to avenge the mighty Queen... Time to avenge them all.

SCARAMOUCHE
The word rhymes with banker!

POP
Get on your bikes and ride!!!

The three of them have mounted up and as the crashing riffs of HEADLONG once more assault and delight the senses, the bike roars into action.

GALILEO
Rock 'n' Roll!!

SCARAMOUCHE
Get down!!

POP
Somebody find me a bat – I want to bite its head off!! – no sleep 'til Hammersmith!

And they sing a chorus of HEADLONG...

> HEADLONG – REPRISE
>
> SCARAMOUCHE, GALILEO, POP
> AND OFFSTAGE CHORUS
> *And you're rushin' headlong*
> *Down the highway*
> *And you're rushin' headlong*
> *Out of control*
> *You think you're so strong*
> *But here ain't no stoppin'*
> *And there's*
> *Nothin' you can, nothin' you can*
> *Nothin' you can do about it!*
>
> *Headlong!*

As the three adventurers journey on the bike the set changes behind them – we see a long virtual journey across time and space, and they finally arrive at... the ruins of Wembley...They get off the bike. They are alone. It is cold and bleak... the wind blows. A desolate wasteland. Nothing but rubble and rubbish. It is miserable. Galileo is very brought down.

POP
Excuse me while I park the bike!

Pop waves his hands to send the bike down the trap.

GALILEO
There's nothing here. Nothing at all.

POP
Bummer.

GALILEO
No instruments, not even any rock.

POP
Just rubble.

GALILEO
This place must have been destroyed centuries ago. It's no Place of Champions anymore if it ever was. I've failed, Scaramouche. I don't know where the Holy Axe is hidden and I will never play the lost riffs. My dreams never come true.

SCARAMOUCHE
Don't blame yourself Gazza, it isn't your fault.

GALILEO
Thanks, Scaramouche.

SCARAMOUCHE
No, I mean it's not your fault you're spineless, gutless, whinging little cry baby!

GALILEO
Excuse me?

SCARAMOUCHE
I know why you can't find the guitar, mate. You remember what Pop said? "Queen wove deep and terrible spells to protect the instruments from those not worthy of playing them."

GALILEO
You mean me?

POP
Ouch!

SCARAMOUCHE
What do you think the Mighty Queen died for? So that you can act like a pathetic little coward! You wanted to be a rock star? Huh! They wouldn't even have you in a boy band!

POP
Ooh!

GALILEO
Hey Babe! I'm getting kind of tired of the self righteous thing OK? We tried, we failed. The instruments are not here. Get over it.

SCARAMOUCHE
Then we'll have to make music without them!

GALILEO
You mean a cappella?

POP
No!

SCARAMOUCHE
If necessary.

POP
It's never necessary!

SCARAMOUCHE
That's what it was all about in the beginning wasn't it? Kids doing it for themselves! Playing in the streets! In the garages!

POP
Yes! Yes! It was!

SCARAMOUCHE
So come on Gazza, where's the bloke I used to love? Where's the bloke with the lead in his pencil? Where is Shagileo Gigolo?

GALILEO
Right here, Babe!

SCARAMOUCHE
Well prove it then – are we gonna rock – or what?

GALILEO
Yes! Yes we are! I don't need some old second-hand instruments to make music. I can do it myself! The music of a human being, not a machine.

SCARAMOUCHE
Right on!

POP
Hello Wembley!!

GALILEO
But... Not without you Scaramouche. You remember what Britney Spears said before he died? Making music is about love... you do it for your Baby... and I can only do it for you. I love you, Scaramouche, with all my heart. Please forgive me. Please come back to me because if you don't, I don't know if I can do this thing, and the kids will be forever in chains.

SCARAMOUCHE
God! Talk about emotional blackmail.

She grabs him and they have a huge snog.

POP
Ooh, I've gone all tingly.

SCARAMOUCHE
So – let's Rock!

Galileo is trying, vainly seeking to summon up inspiration from within. He is truly ready but it is not easy... He is tense... desperate, trying to summon up the spirit...

GALILEO
I... don't know how to start...

Scaramouche is egging him on.

SCARAMOUCHE
Come on Buddy! You're a boy...

Pop also tries to encourage Galileo.

POP
Make a big noise!

SCARAMOUCHE
Playing in the street!

POP
Gonna be a big man some day...

GALILEO
Hey! Hey that's it!!...

SCARAMOUCHE
What is?

Tentatively Galileo echoes their words, but as a chant....

GALILEO

B... B... Buddy... Buddy you're a boy... make a big noise... Playing in the street gonna be a big man some day...

POP

What a curiously exhilarating collection of words.

Now Galileo is really summoning it up. He pauses, then he begins to stamp the ground to gather his strength and continues.

GALILEO

You got mud on your face. You big disgrace. Kickin' your can all over the place.

Now something magical happens. Now in the distance the arcane beat of the WE WILL ROCK YOU stamps and claps can be heard.

It is the audience!!!

The beat grows huge, and Galileo pitches in for real. Galileo the Rock Star!

GALILEO (cont'd)

Listen Scaramouche. It's the beat! The beat is returning.

SCARAMOUCHE

The beating of our hearts!

GALILEO

Hearts of solid rock!

Now Galileo sings and performs with an infectious and rapidly growing confidence.

WE WILL ROCK YOU

GALILEO

Buddy you're a boy, make a big noise
Playing in the street, gonna be big man some day
You got mud on yo' face
You big disgrace
Kickin' your can all over the place
Singin'
We will, we will rock you
We will, we will rock you
We will, we will...

Now more magic happens. Something fabulous!

A huge guitar chord from WE WILL ROCK YOU rips through the air and, as it does so, a great pile of rubble collapses.

From the ruins of Wembley Stadium emerges... a GUITAR! Half embedded in the rock!

SCARAMOUCHE

What's happening?

POP

Thunderbolt and lightning, very, very frightening!

GALILEO

Scaramouche! Look! An instrument! A musical instrument!

SCARAMOUCHE

So they exist after all!

POP

The dream machine! The most powerful weapon of freedom known to man! An "electric guitar"! Seize it Shagileo Gigolo, for none but the just shall play the Hairy One's Mighty Axe. None but the Kids!

SCARAMOUCHE

Wow! You're my guitar hero!

GALILEO

Yes I am, Baby! And now! Let's Rock!

He tries to play it but is complete crap.

POP

Oh no man! The rebirth of modern jazz!

SCARAMOUCHE

I thought you were really good Gaz... No, really!

Scaramouche grabs the guitar and rips off a couple of killer chords and a significant bit of diddling.

GALILEO

The Hairy One is back, and this time – she's a babe!

SCARAMOUCHE

So I'll play, you sing.

GALILEO

Yeah!

POP

And I'll be a groupie. Anyone want to see my tits?

SCARAMOUCHE

Shut up, Pop!

POP

Received and understood, but first...

Pop whips out a little communicator.

GALILEO

What are you doing, Pop?

POP

What do you think? Hacking into the Globalsoft mainframe and e-mailing the Power of Rock to every Ga Ga Kid on the Planet. Soon they'll all be Bohemians.

SCARAMOUCHE

But Pop, the Killer Queen will get your e-mail too!

Pop glances at his modem.

POP

Oh no, Man, she just did!

The Royal screen descends, and an irate Killer Queen appears.

KILLER QUEEN
Who dares play live rock music on Planet Mall?

THE BAND
We do, Killer Queen – all right?!!!

KILLER QUEEN
What?

THE BAND
Shagileo Gigolo's Band!

KILLER QUEEN
Who?

GALILEO
Did you hear that, Scaramouche? I've got a band... now the Kids can see the true Power of Rock.

POP
Well not all of them actually... most of the kids can only see half of the true Power of Rock and then only the tops of their heads.

GALILEO
Well, the top of the heads of half of the Power of Rock is enough to vanquish Globalsoft. Boys – unleash the Mighty Riffs, and tie that Mother down!

The band unleash the power riffs of

TIE YOUR MOTHER DOWN – Killer Queen wants to boogie but screams in horror as she realizes she is being vapourised by the power of Rock!

KILLER QUEEN
No, no, no, no, no...!

Her screen flies out as she disappears for the last time.

GALILEO
Pop, bring me my mike.

POP
I'm a groupie and a roadie! I'll have to have sex with myself! So, no change there then!

SCARAMOUCHE
Shut up Pop!

Pop collects the mike stand for Galileo.

POP
One two... One two...

The entire company of Bohemians now reappear. They are rejuvenated, and in a state of ecstatic grace. They have been drawn by the music... It is almost like some ancient pagan religious gathering... Gazza smashes back into the song.

We Will Rock You

GALILEO AND THE KIDS

Buddy you're a boy, make a big noise
Playin' in the street, gonna be a big man some day
You got mud on yo' face
You big disgrace
Kickin' your can all over the place
Singin'
We will, we will rock you
We will, we will rock you

Buddy you're a young man, hard man
Shouting in the street, gonna take on the world
*   some day*
You got blood on yo' face
You big disgrace
Wavin' your banner all over the place

We will, we will rock you – ev'rybody
We will, we will rock you

Buddy you're an old man, poor man
Pleadin' with your eyes, gonna make you some
peace some day
You got mud on yo' face
You big disgrace
Somebody better put you back into your place

We will, we will rock you – sing it!
We will, we will rock you
We will, we will rock you
We will, we will rock you

Scaramouche leads the kids into the guitar solo climax of WE WILL ROCK YOU – a big finish. The Holy Axe is ceremonially carried off at head height by Pop.

The lights go down, and we become aware of Galileo at the front, spotlighted on a dark stage. Finally fully in control, he sings…

We Are The Champions

GALILEO AND COMPANY

I've paid my dues time after time
I've done my sentence but committed no crime
And bad mistakes I've made a few
I've had my share of sand kicked in my face
But I've come through
(And I mean to go on and on and on and on)

We are the champions my friends
And we'll keep on fighting to the end
We are the champions
We are the champions
No time for losers 'cos
We are the champions
Of the world

We are the champions my friends
And we'll keep on fighting to the end
We are the champions
We are the champions
No time for losers 'cos
We are the champions
Of the world!!!

Bohemian Rhapsody

The audience (always!) rise to his triumph !!!

WE WILL ROCK YOU (the fast version) almost immediately kicks in, during which the cast take their bows and the band rock out.

> **COMPANY**
> *We will, we will rock you!*
> *We will, we will rock you, rock you, rock you,*
>   *rock you*
> *We will, we will – Rock!*
> *Rock YOU!*

The audience are now asked if they would finally like to hear the Holy Grail of the WWRY story, BOHEMIAN RHAPSODY, in its entirety.
The answer is affirmative.

GALILEO, SCARAMOUCHE, KILLER QUEEN, KHASHOGGI AND THE ENTIRE COMPANY
Mama just killed a man
Put a gun against his head
Pulled my trigger now he's dead
Mama life had just begun
But now I've gone and thrown it all away
Mama ooh
Didn't mean to make you cry
If I'm not back again this time tomorrow
Carry on carry on
As if nothing really matters

Too late my time has come
Sends shivers down my spine
Body's achin' all the time
Goodbye ev'rybody I've got to go
Gotta leave you all behind and face the truth

Mama ooh
(Any way the wind blows)
I don't wanna die
I sometimes wish I'd never been born at all

Spotlight guitar solo

I see a little silhouetto of a man Scaramouche
Scaramouche will do the Fandango
Thunderbolt and light'ning
Very very fright'ning me
Galileo Galileo Galileo
Galileo Galileo Figaro
Magnifico-o-o-o-o
I'm just a poor boy
Nobody loves me
He's just a poor boy from a poor family
Spare him his life from this monstrosity
Easy come easy go
Will you let me go
Bismillah! No!
We will not let you go
Let him go
Bismillah!
We will not
Let him go
We will not let you go
Let me go
Will not let you go
Let me go
Never never never never
Let me go-o-o-o-o
No no no no no no no
Oh mama mia mama mia
Mama mia let me go
Beelzebub has a devil put aside for me
For me, for me!

Heavy instrumental break (The *Wayne's World* bit!)

So you think you can stone me and spit in my eye
So you think you can love me and leave me to die
Oh baby

Can't do this to me baby
Just gotta get out
Just gotta get right outta here

Ooh Ooh yeah
Nothing really matters
Anyone can see
Nothing really matters
Nothing really matters to me
Any way the wind blows

Of course at the end, after all the huge noise and lights and smoke, it all returns to just Galileo and Scaramouche alone in the darkness for the last time. Galileo lingers on his own to sing

Nothing really matters to me.

But then Scara holds out her hand for him to follow, and he joins her. They embrace.

Finally even they disappear into the dark. Only Galileo's voice is left.

Anyway the wind blows...

Curtain